A Player's Eyes

One Man's View of Sexual Relationships

A Player's Eyes

One Man's View of Sexual Relationships

Rom Wills

Wills Publishing

A Player's Eyes
One Man's View of Sexual Relationships

Copyright © 2015
By
Romuald P. Wills

Romuald P. Wills
romwills@aol.com

ISBN-13   978-0692553770
ISBN-10 0692553770

To my sons.

Also by Rom Wills

Nice Guys and Players
Sexual Chemistry
Meeting Attractive Women
Finding the Right Man
Starting From Zero
The Sankofans
Those Eyes

Every saint has a past.
Every sinner has a future.

-   Unknown

Table of Contents

I am a Player

I am a Player. I am a Ladies' Man, Casanova, Mack, Chick Magnet, Loverman, Womanizer, Lothario, Rake, Dog, Bad Boy, and Romeo. Colorful names thrown around by those looking from the outside in. Terms used to describe a man they do not and cannot understand. For many years I cringed when the terms were applied to me. "No, no," I would protest. "I'm a good guy," I would say to countless people who would use these terms to describe their perception of me. "No," I would protest as I would catch eyes with a young woman with a pretty face and ass shaped like an upside down heart. "I'm one of the nice guys," I would say as the young woman next to her with breasts served up in a double D bra would shyly lower her eyes and then look up coyly with a slight smile on her face. "I'm not a player," I would say as a slim woman with her booty poking

11

out just right walks up to me and puts a business card into my coat pocket.

For real I was just in denial. I am what I am. I'm a man who loves the ladies and a man the ladies loves back. What can I say? It's good to be me.

For many I'm the villain of the story. Jealous men and jilted women have thrown shade my way over the years. The men mad that the women they sweated, wined, dined, and chased for years showed me love when all I did was say hi and maybe held the door for them. Jilted women mad at me because despite their seductive best I wasn't feeling their flavor. Hey a brotha got standards. Whatever. I never worried about these folks though. As long as they didn't have a gun in their hands (and I've had guns in my face) I wasn't worried. It's all part of the game of life. I've lost women I've wanted to other men and I've been rejected. It is what it is.

I have no regrets. I have been in various types of relationships with women from all over the world. I have been with women young and old, rich and poor, drop dead gorgeous, and those with faces that only a mother could truly love. I have had one night stands, relationships lasting a few days, weeks, months, and even years as I was married to the mother of my sons. Those were just the relationships where sexual intimacy was a part of the equation whether it was a quickie in a storage room or hours long lovemaking at a bed and breakfast. Many of my most satisfying encounters with the female gender were simply times where the intimacy

12

consisted of a stimulating conversation, or receiving sage advice from one of several mother figures, or getting tough love from female friends who wanted the best for me.

Being a Player isn't always about sex. I have a lot of female friends. To this day I can call up most of my ex-girlfriends and sex partners and shoot the breeze. I love the energy of women period. To me it makes life worth living. True Players know what I'm talking about.

So why am I writing this? See it's not about me. I provided the little bit above to set the tone. To let the reader know where I'm coming from. The reason I call this piece, "A Player's Eyes."

Since the mid 1990's I have written several books and articles talking about male/female relationships. My focus has been primarily on self-development for both men and women. My thought is that if someone wants to have better relationships they need to improve themselves. Many men and women complain about the opposite sex but will not look in the mirror and deal with their own issues. If somebody doesn't want you it's because of **YOU**. It's not that women don't want a "good man." It's **YOU** women don't want. It's not that men don't want a "good woman." It's **YOU** men don't want. All of my books encourage self-improvement. I constantly practice what I preach. One of the reasons I've had so much success with women is because I've had so many failures. Instead of becoming bitter I would simply look at what **I** did wrong. Even in cases where the other party did some foul shit. I would check myself for

13

going along for with the bull. No women has ever held a gun to my head. One time I dealt with a game playing drama queen who played me a couple of times. I didn't get mad at her. I look at myself and searched for what it was within me that would fall for the same bullshit twice. After dealing with the particular issue I never got played that same way again. I learn from my mistakes. I encourage as much in my books, articles, and coaching.

I've done several relationship panels, seminars, radio, and cable shows. I've noticed one thing, which is why I avoid doing media now unless I know the host of show will allow my voice to be free. Most people in attending these seminars don't want solutions. They are looking for somebody to cosign their point of view. Women are looking for someone to say that there is indeed a "shortage of good men" or "that all men are dogs." Men, when they do show up to these seminars, want to know why women are passing them over for "bad boys." When I start talking some real talk the women would get mad and the men would be ready to fight. I was actually threatened with bodily harm at one panel for saying that many men like natural hair on a woman. The irony was that at the time this wasn't my sentiment. I was simply repeating what I was told by several men. It was a case of shooting the messenger. After a while I got tired of the bullshit. So with all that said why this book?

God, or whatever term someone wants to use, Jesus, Allah, Ausar, Shango, Buddha, or the Great Pumpkin, put it on my heart to say something.

14

Now let's make something very clear. I'm going to talk about certain issues from my perspective. Not somebody else's perspective. I'm not going to quote a bunch of studies which are quite frankly of dubious validity. I'm going to look at different things from the perspective of the Player that I am. Most of what I'm going to be talking about will be dealing with real life sexual dynamics. One of the biggest problems in relationship discussions is that sex is left out of the conversation. Now some folks will do seminars and workshops on how to have sex. I know several people who conduct Tantric sex workshops. These folks mainly deal with the mechanics of sexual intercourse. Yet few people will talk about how a person's desire for sex with a particular person will affect their relationship choices. Much of what I will talk about will deal with sexual politics. To put it in the vernacular of those of more roughhewn sensibilities: I'm going to break the game down. In my fifty odd years of life I've seen many things. I share my perspective not to say I have the best way, or the right way. I share my perspective to give the reader something to think about. At the end of the day that all we can do. There's no right and wrong. It is what it is. Just to be clear I'm going to be raw because I want the reader to feel the emotion of what I'm writing. So expect to see a curse word or two. I'm coming from the heart with this and won't be politically correct just to ease someone's sensibilities. That out of the way I invite the reader to see the world through "A Player's Eyes."

The Sexual Nature of a Woman

When I was seven years old my uncle came by the house to take me to church. My uncle was the coolest, smoothest dude I knew in my brief life up to that point. He was a police detective who rolled like Shaft and looked like Billy Dee Williams. Denzel Washington's character, Alonzo Harris, from the movie *Training Day* had nothing on my uncle. So when he got to the house he looked at me and was visibly disappointed. My hair wasn't combed. Before we left he made sure my hair was right and then we left for church. In the car he let me have it. He actually raised his voice to me. He talked about the importance of looking good. He then asked if I had a girlfriend. I told him no. I'm thinking to myself that I'm seven, what I need with a girlfriend. He told me if I had a girlfriend she would break up with me for looking so raggedy. That was one of my earliest lessons in the game of boy gets girl. The lesson was that looks matter to women.

In the popular culture and indeed in conventional beliefs there is the notion that looks don't matter to women as much as they do with men. Even when women do say that looks matter they will put it low on the list of priorities of what they want in a man. I'm throwing a flag on that. Fifteen yard penalty for unsportsmanlike bullshit. The reality is that not only do looks matter but they matter more to women than they do to men. This is especially true in sexual matters. When women look for long term partners such as boyfriends and husbands they will look at personality compatibility, social class, money, religious affiliation, political views, education level, and even something as trivial as music tastes. The trick though is that they look for these things in men they find **PHYSICALLY** attractive. When women say that there is a shortage of "good men" what they really mean is that there is a shortage of "good **LOOKING** men."

The looks women want in a man isn't just about aesthetics. It's about how a woman's body reacts to the physical nature of a particular man. Women already know what I'm talking about. For the man reading this think about it like this. How often has your dick got hard from seeing a woman with big breasts? Or a nice juicy phat ass? Or long shapely legs? Women are the exact same way. I've seen women go into trances because they saw a man with a big chest and big arms. Some women lose their mind if they see the calves on a man. Many women struggle to keep their

17

composure if they see a man's dick print and it looks like he is packing. Let me give some game here and not that bullshit that passes as game on the Internet being taught by men who can count the number of women they've had sex with on one hand. A woman can have an orgasm just from **LOOKING** at a man.

I had a friend years ago. She was what is known in urban communities as a freak. The more general term now would be "thot," – "that hoe over there" for those not hip to contemporary slang. Yeah whatever. To me she was a sexually open woman with whom I engaged in phone sex with every now and then because she lived in another state. We would talk with each other in general about our sexual experiences. I remember we were talking one evening and she described a man she saw at a gas station. She said, "Rom this man's aura was so strong that when I saw him I had to sit down on the curb." Just from looking at this man she reacted as if she just had some good dick. Keep in mind that this man didn't say one word to her. He might not have noticed her. Many women do this. They will see a man and something in them will shift. Over the years I've seen women stop in their tracks when they saw certain men. Reportedly if a woman's pupils dilate, her cervix will contract. The contraction of the cervix is one type of orgasm a woman can have. Are you making the connection?

When a woman looks at a man she looks for sexual worthiness. Many women will publically admit that they know within a few seconds of meeting a man whether or not they will have sex with him. They will put him into a Select or Non-Select category. If she puts him into the Select category she will give him a chance to seduce her. At that point the man needs to avoid saying or doing anything stupid. If she puts him into the Non-Select category there is nothing he can do to seduce her. Even in those rare cases where a Non-Select man manages to get the girl so to speak he will find that she will treat him in an inferior way. Sex gets rationed and she will likely cheat as soon as a buffed pretty boy decides to return her texts.

Now when I say sexual worthiness a woman is looking at a man's body build, his face to see if he is kissable, and even how he moves. To put it in the terms of a young woman I knew back in the day, "Is he fuckable?" Many men approach a woman thinking that if they say the right combination of words, make her laugh, or in some cases put her down they can seduce her. Sorry Charlie, that woman made her decision within five seconds of seeing you. If she talks to you anyway it's more for her entertainment, and the number you just got may be fake, and if it's real she'll ignore your texts.

I'm sorry I had to be the one to tell you.

Some men are still going to be in denial of what I just wrote. Even some sexually repressed women. I'll get to the men in second. I've made an observation about women who say looks don't matter. If they are not outright lying they are sexually repressed and honestly believe what they are saying. I've noticed one thing in talking with these women over the years. Well let me back up a bit. My smooth uncle taught me a lot about how to get information out of people. When he talked to crime suspects they would confess to crimes that he didn't arrest them for. He would catch them for one thing and they would tell him about fifteen more crimes. His secret was that he would get them so comfortable they would become chatterboxes. I watched him growing up as he dealt with people so I learned the same skills. As an aside, old school players didn't give seminars or have online videos. The only way to learn from them was if they let you hang around them. They rarely told you anything directly. With the sexually repressed women I would get them so comfortable around me they would tell me some interesting things. For them looks definitely mattered but the more repressed a woman is the more perfect a man has to be to turn her on sexually. Indeed one will find with these women that they tend not to have boyfriends or even a good maintenance man. They will tend to have a lot of males as platonic friends. Are you going to tell me that at least one of these men doesn't have the personality characteristics she says are important? Think on this.

Men are in denial because of one major thing. The average man knows he is just that, average. A man can look in the mirror and can see he isn't the tallest man, or the most muscular. The average man knows he isn't going to make money with his face. Over the centuries men would focus on what they could control which was their ability to provide for a woman, their ability to protect a woman, and their ability to talk to a woman. What developed was the false belief that a man's physical appearance wasn't as important. It was always important to a woman but it was also important that she had food in her stomach. Women had to attach themselves to the man most willing to take care of them. What's changed is that women don't need a man to survive anymore. They can get their own money now and pay for what's needed for survival. Women still need good dick though. Take away the "protect and provide" angle and the fuckable aspect of a man becomes more prominent. What has happened is that women are free to go after men based on nothing else but pure lust. Many men are still stuck in that 1950's paradigm. Feminism and the sexual revolution took care of that. Now there are still women who look for a man to protect and provide for them but they are looking for him in buffed package.

Some men are reading this and are still going to be in denial. They will say something to the effect of money and being able to talk to women with "good game" as being more important than looks. They are still important, but they are secondary concerns. Some women don't even care about those things. There are plenty of kept men out there. I've known a few such men in my day. The women will work on some high paying job and the role of the man was simply to stay looking good and fuck the woman's brains out when she got home. That's just the underground shit. The maintenance man game is a street hustle not talked about on the Internet and in most relationship forums and seminars.

The most public equivalent are male escorts who advertise on the Internet. Knowing an actual street gigolo is roughly the equivalent of knowing real hitman. Yeah it's that deep. That may be another book. Just to let you know that I'm not talking out the side of my neck about a woman's sexual nature being more visual I'm going to provide a few real life examples which anyone of reasonable intelligence can explore on their own.

Let me share a story with you. When my book, *Nice Guys and Players*, was first published I sold several copies at an expo back in 2000. My girlfriend and I set up my vending table. As we were setting up we noticed that some very muscular brothas were setting up across from us. Their only product was calendars with their pictures in them. Maybe three other groups of muscular brothas set up near us as well. It turns out that these men were exotic dancers. What happened over the next two days confirmed what I had written in my book. Women were packed in our little section of the convention center where the expo was held. In addition to me and the dancers a photographer had set up a booth to take pictures. He stayed busy as young and old women would drag different dancers over to take pictures with them. Over the years I have known male strippers who made drug dealer type money. Half of them really can't dance. There are videos on the Internet of women making it rain for male dancers. I've known about groups of women who would rent out hotel rooms and pay several thousand dollars for dancers to entertain them. They were doing more than dancing. These men weren't there because of their financial portfolios or their stimulating conversations. These women wanted their bodies.

Another example is sex tourism. There's a lot of talk of men going on sex vacations to different parts of the world. Many people publically act disgusted by the practice. What's not talked about is that women engage in sex tourism just as much if not more than men. There's been some videos about women going to places like Jamaica and Kenya as sex tourists. That's been going on for years. I first heard about women being sex tourists in the mid-eighties from women who engaged in the practice. In the late-eighties I knew several men from the Caribbean who said they "knew" men who catered to tourists. It's an unofficial economic engine in some places. Once again these women are not going for a stimulating convo. They want a man with a tight ass body. Women pay for what they value. If they weren't turned on sexually by a man's body there wouldn't be male strippers and many Caribbean islands would have to replace a major economic driver.

Go in any major bookstore to the romance section. The male protagonists in these books aren't soft body fellows with good hearts and lots of money. Whether the male romantic interest is a biker or a billionaire with issues the men are always described as physically attractive. If women weren't turned on by a man's looks the covers to romance novels would look very different. Many books have sold copies for no other reason than that there was a handsome

23

man on the cover.   On the cover to my book, *Sexual Chemistry,* I used a picture of myself wearing a wife beater. I was told by one of my distributors that many WOMEN bought the book, which is primarily directed at men, because of the picture.   I did a book signing one time and a woman kissed the cover of one of my books and then tried to kiss me!

The final example I want to use may make people squeamish but it has to be said because not publically recognizing that women are sexually aroused by visual cues can have serious emotional repercussions for many men. Every week it seems there is some story about a female teacher being convicted of sleeping with an underaged boy. Now people may say the women were mentally sick or some other excuse that ignores the obvious.   These women slept with these young boys because the young boys looked good to them.   Every other explanation is bullshit and is best left to defense attorneys who are trying to keep their clients out of prison.   In many of these cases the teachers didn't just rape some young boy.   In most cases these teachers were in relationships with these boys.   These are just the teachers. Every neighborhood has at least one woman who the smart mothers in that area keep an eye on.   A woman knows when somebody is looking at her baby boy in that way.   Since the sixth grade at any given time I knew at least one teenage boy who was getting his dick sucked by a woman old enough to be his mother.   This is a game my Grandmother hipped me to so I know all about it.   I pay close attention whenever an older woman is around my sons. I will publically debate any man or woman on this issue because it's personal for me. That's all you need to know.

These older women ain't getting with these young boys to be provided for and protected. What a teenaged boy have to offer a grown-ass woman? He doesn't have any resources. He's still sleeping in same bunk bed he's had for years. He doesn't have that thing called "game." Real game is knowledge about life. A teenager regardless of how mature he may be otherwise only has limited life experience. He can't game a grown-ass woman who has reasonable intelligence. The young boy has one trump card and one trump card only with the older woman: his body. Regardless of how a woman wants to rationalize the situation a young boy really has nothing else to offer.

The bottom line with all of this is that it's the very nature of women to be turned on sexually by simply looking at a man. Looks matter and a man's "look" matters. Not only are women are looking at a man's body build, and facial features but are checking out his overall appearance. Women are checking out a man's haircut, his facial hair grooming, his clothes, his jewelry, and especially his shoes. I'm going to play the race card here. Being fit and looking fly has been the base of the game learned in Black communities for decades. It's still there. There's a BIG difference between what passes as game on white male dominated Internet forums and taught in expensive seminars and what a Black kid in Chicago or Washington DC will know.   What the inner city kid knows is that it's about the look.   If a woman doesn't like a man's look there is very little he can do to get her.   This knowledge is shared in my books.

A Goodbar's World

I was at a hair show a few years ago doing what I do which is sell books. The way it was set up there were some women standing a few feet behind me talking. I didn't pay much attention to them as they didn't seem interested in what I was selling. No biggie. As they were talking a big muscular dude walked by. I had seen him earlier as he bought a copy of my book *Nice Guys and Players*. Even though he didn't look like he needed the book he bought it anyway. Men who need my books the least buy them the quickest. As he walked by one of the women behind me called out to him, "Can I take you home?" Without saying anything he walked over to her, took out his phone, handed it to her and said, "Put your number in my phone." She complied. He looked at the phone, "Is that it?" She nodded yes. Without saying another word he walked off. She looked at me and said, "A

27

sista has to be aggressive." I laughed with her. I've seen this scenario in one form or another dozens of times. It was another view of a Goodbar's world.

Earlier I spoke of how women put men into two different categories in terms of sexual desirability: Select and Non-Select. I talk about this in my books, blogs, and videos. The Select Men are the sexually desirable men and the Non-Select are undesirable men. There are sub-categories within the categories. Within the Select group there are the men known as Mr. Goodbars and the Masked Men. The Mr. Goodbars are the men with raw sex appeal be it an extremely handsome face, killer body, or off the chains sexual charisma. The Masked Men are the men who are generically handsome with above average money and/or status. The Non-Select group includes the Nice Guys who are mainly Average Joes and the Gamesmen who think they have game but in reality are just persistent in chasing women. I talk about the different groups in my books and blogs quite enough. I focus right now on the Goodbars. I want to share their perspective of the world.

I remember one time I was talking with this man back in the nineties. He was saying how he had spent $400 on dates with a young lady but still hadn't had sex with her. The 2015 equivalent is probably $800 or more. I listened to him and nodded at appropriate times. The whole time I was thinking that the concept of spending that much money just to get sex was alien to me. I've gone to hotels where the women paid for the room. Instead of going out on dates I

28

got invited over to a woman's house or apartment. I think the most I probably spent on a woman up to that point was $30 and that was **AFTER** having sex with them. I had problems paying for the company of a woman. The reason was that I knew a man didn't have to pay for their company. If a woman wants to be around a man she'll go walk through the park with him and be good. Then again there is that double standard. If a woman is sexually turned on by a man she will simply want to be around him. If she isn't she may go on an expensive date with him but at the end of the night all he may get is a kiss on the cheek and a brother/sister type hug. That's if she had a good time.

The dating scene is different for a Goodbar. He doesn't have to approach several women on the street hoping that one will not only stop and talk but also give him the correct number and return the text within an hour. Usually women are either making it extremely easy for Goodbar to approach them or they simply take the initiative and find an excuse to approach Goodbar.

Here's the thing. There are many physically desirable women. One thing with women is that as a group more of them will actively cultivate their physical sex appeal. There are whole industries that cater to this. You have the cosmetics industry, the hair industry, the clothing industry, and even the shoe industry. The only functional purpose of high heel shoes is to magnify a woman's butt and legs to make her look sexier. High heel shoes really aren't good for women otherwise. Indeed women with naturally shapely legs tend not to wear them.

On the other side of the coin men as a group do not cultivate their physical sex appeal to the same extent. The average man will let his body grow soft and will keep the same hair cut for years. As a group men don't dress well. A friend pointed out to me that other than a college football town you don't see that many muscular men walking around. Even rarer are going to be men with extremely handsome faces. Now let's think about some things.

Women are turned on by a man's looks which includes his face, body, and overall appearance. Only a small percentage of men have sexually appealing looks. This is something women **WANT**. So when they **SEE** it they tend to be more aggressive about approaching that man. If that man decides to approach them they will be extremely receptive to what he has to say. She could have fifteen men trying to date her but she will clear her calendar for this man. If she has a boyfriend or husband she may cheat with Goodbar. If Goodbar says he needs $500 to get his car out of the shop he will likely get the money. Yeah it's that deep. This is why male exotic dancers make so much money. If women saw physically attractive men on a regular basis they wouldn't feel the need to make it rain in a club. They wouldn't feel the need to sleep with a student in their class or their nice young neighbor who cuts the grass.

People may think Goodbar has it made. Maybe. Yes a Goodbar gets more chances with women. Yes he is the man that a supermodel will stalk. With the good comes the bad. A Goodbar can have a sincere interest in a woman but if she is insecure there will be problems. Also many women do not want to be with a man who looks better than they do. One of the main reasons Goodbars buy my book the most is because I have advice for a man who normally attracts many women, but can't get the woman he wants. The back cover of *Nice Guys and Players* asks the question, "Are you a player who can get every woman except the one you love?" Of course I got a story behind this one.

I was doing a book signing at a mall kiosk. I was sitting there chilling with a few people when this Hispanic man came walking up. I kid you not, it was like a spotlight was on him. He walked up with an entourage. I swear I heard theme music. This dude was looking good, no homo. His haircut was on point. He had on a silk shirt and some nice slacks that looked like they were from a high-end store. His Italian shoes was shined to the point where a brotha could see his reflection. He walked up, grabbed a book, read the back and said with flair, "Now this is who I am! I can get every woman except the one I want! How much is this book?" I ain't going lie, the dude had so much charisma dripping off of him I almost gave him the book for free. Almost. His boys bought copies too.

Other than finding the one special woman, a Goodbar has no real concept of chasing women. Now Gamesmen types who approach several women a day may think they are better at getting women than Goodbar since

31

they are more aggressive in approaching. Naw. Goodbar may have trouble getting the one he really wants but he's consoled by what he does get.

The average man doesn't have even a concept of what it's like to be pursued by women to say nothing about very beautiful women. If a man is pursued he can just sit back and choose which woman he wants to entertain at any given moment. If a woman really wants him she may bring a plate of food. That's why many desirable men will act arrogant and spoiled. Women are giving them the goodies without them having to do anything other than keeping their hair right and doing daily pushups.

One thing I've noticed over the past several years is that there are several relationship experts who are also Goodbars. They never have anything negative to say about women and indeed most of their work caters to women. Many Non-Select men resent this. They feel like these relationship experts are selling out the brotherhood. Not really. These men just do not have the same relationship experience with women. From a personal point of view even though I will call out women on foul behavior, for the most part I get nothing but support. When I call them on things it's never personal but truly tough love. Even platonically women have always been cool with me and they have always showed me love. Even though I've been rejected by women it was never a thing of constant rejection. Even then the rejections were never mean spirited except for one time. Indeed I've actually had women change their mind about me because I was cool with them even when things didn't become romantic.   Things would heat up later on. The few times I was friendzoned I never stayed there.

Non-Select Men can learn a lot from Goodbars. One thing I've noticed is that Select and Non-Select men really don't interact with each other.   It is literally two different worlds.   Non-Select men usually paint Select men particularly Goodbars as pretty boys and bad boys.   Non-Select men usually attack women and call them stupid for being attracted to such men.   It's a stupid move on both counts.   Women are going to be attracted to who they going to be attracted to regardless of what any man wants or thinks.   Most men can improve their physical appearance if they are willing to do the work.   As far as other things, here's a secret. The best way for a man to come close to being a Goodbar is to simply hang out around one.   Instead trying to put down the Goodbar, Non-Select men need to befriend them when they encounter one.   It can make a big difference in their lives because it will change how a Non-Select man thinks.

Until Non-Select men change their thinking it will always be a Goodbar's World.

A Woman's Game

One thing I find really fascinating is the concept of game as it is shared on Internet forums, blogs, and videos. You have an "expert," in many cases someone who looks like they've seen no parts of the pussy, telling clueless men how to get laid. Not only get laid but laid with very beautiful women. There's a whole industry for this. My books and blogs are considered part of this industry even though I don't actually teach "game" as many detractors have pointed out. I even did a blog series on why I don't teach game.

I check out the theories and philosophies of different teachers. A few have useful advice. Most are wack. I've had several coaching clients over the years who had embraced these teachings. I usually spent initial coaching sessions deprogramming my clients because quite frankly they picked up some bad habits which needed to be dealt with before I could teach them anything useful. For those wondering what I do, I really just change a man or woman's thinking. I give them a new way of looking at relationships. In successful cases they find that they were like Dorothy from the *Wizard of Oz*, they had the power all along. I wake people up to their own potential. The successful ones anyway. Quite a few wanted to stay asleep and that's their right.

Getting back to that thing called game, one issue I have is that men really think they are gaming women. They're not. Game is really to build a man's confidence. Women are going to choose who they want. Game as it is generally shared in the public sphere doesn't work on women. Men think it works on women but on the for real for real, women just let men think it works. When a man approaches a woman, she has already decided what she's going to do with him. If she wants to have sex with him she has already decided to do so. Now if he wants to throw some corny lines at her, make a production of getting her phone number, take her on an expensive date, and let him think he convinced her to take her panties down, far be it for her to spoil his illusion. She'll let him think he has control when in reality she's been in total control the whole time.

A key component of "game" shared on the Internet is approaching women. Indeed many seminars are given in order to build up a man's confidence in order to approach. Here's the problem with that. Any true Player, Playboy, Pimp, Mack, anybody who's learned the "game" in the streets through trial and error will tell you not to approach a woman who has not chosen you. A true to the game Player is not going to approach a woman who has not given a clear indication that she wants to be approached. When a woman wants to be approached by a particular man they have their tricks to entice him. I talk about some of these things in my book, *Nice Guys and Players*. If a woman chooses a man she is already receptive to whatever he has to say. He just has to be smart enough not to blow the opportunity. Now when a man approaches a woman who has not chosen him she will not be receptive to him regardless of what combination of words is coming out of his mouth. The best thing that can happen for the man is that she ignores him. The worst that can happen is if she stops and seems receptive to what he has to say. It's even worse if she gives him her number and responds quickly to his texts. This seems like a good thing. Naw. Dude is about to get played.

Let me share something about me. I learned a whole lot from old school players growing up. The only thing was that all of these players were not men. I got definite gems from some men but the most useful information came from women. Not just any women. I learned from sex workers, strippers, freelance prostitutes, street walking prostitutes, a couple of call girls, true to the game gold diggers and a few sugar babies. Throw in more than a few unrepentant promiscuous women and some MILFs and cougars and I had an interesting education. As a result of spending a portion of my life in an extremely dysfunctional environment I'm comfortable around people who don't quite fit into respectable society. I could be around one of these women and they could tell me they just engaged in group sex with eight men or just had a stranger pay them $500 for sex and I would react the same way I would if they told me it was sunny outside. These women would not only confide in me but give me tips on how to get a woman to suck my dick. There's no such thing as a sisterhood. Women are very competitive with each other. Publically a woman will embrace another woman and call her sister and say they are standing against the Patriarchy or something. Privately that woman will let the husband of the woman she just embraced have anal sex with her.

The main thing I learned is that women control the game. The way they control it is that men will approach them without being chosen. When a man approaches a woman without being seduced to do so the woman has total control of the situation. Think about it, the man is trying to get something from the woman, likely sex. The woman knows this unless she's a social idiot. The woman has something the man wants. She then can decide on the **PRICE** a man has to pay to get sex. The woman will **NEVER** tell the man the **PRICE**. Here's the game. She can now use him by dangling the bait of pussy in front of his face. She can get money, gifts, concert tickets, clothes, and even some of her bills paid. I knew one woman who had a man who would give her money every time he got paid. I asked her if she gave him any pussy. She said, "Rom, if I did that he wouldn't give me money anymore." We were real cool though, she made sure my pockets stayed blessed. A true Street Cat knows what I'm talking about with that last statement.

I saw a quote one time that said, "A man chases a woman until she catches him." A man thinks he's gaming a woman by chasing her when really she's gaming him. Women are smart because they'll use a man's nature against him. Too many men think they can convince a woman to like them. Many don't have the discipline to sit back and let a woman try to seduce them. Many men don't like the idea that a particular woman may not want them. The thing is maybe a particular woman doesn't want them but two other women who may be better in looks and compatibility will want the man. A man doesn't need game to get a woman. A man simply needs to pay attention. It's been my observation that regardless of how a man looks, talks, and smells there's a least one decent woman who wants to fuck him. He just needs to be on the lookout for her.

One aspect of the Woman's game I want to address is this notion that there is a shortage of men. There is indeed a shortage of the men women collectively find desirable. That being said the average looking woman usually has several men. She might have to share some of those men but they are still available to her. As I mentioned before women place men into two general categories, Select and Non-Select. These are just general terms. Every **SINGLE** woman has their own personal criteria for men and how she will deal with them. Men have harems, women have rosters. An average looking woman will have about five men.   Now before someone wants to object to this characterization I'm speaking in general terms.   If you are a woman reading this and what I say doesn't apply to you, keep it moving.   I'm willing to bet every woman has at least one "friend" to whom this applies.   Let's break this down according level of significance to a woman starting from the lowest to the highest.

The first man a woman has is the Thirsty Man.   The Thirsty Man is the one she gave her number to or friended on social media.   This is the dude who will like all of her pictures even the one that showed a booger hanging out her nose.   This is the dude who will blow up her inbox if she even hints that she is having a bad day.   This is the dude who will send five long ass texts, and when she responds in two hours with a one word answer he sends her two more long texts.   This the dude that hits her up late at night even though they've never been on a date and she's given no indication that she wants to give him anything other than a firm handshake.   She keeps him around though for an ego boost.   He'll never get to see her panties.

The next man a woman has is the Friendzone Guy. She's way cooler with the Friendzone Guy.   She'll return his texts promptly and will respond to his comments on social media.   She'll even hang out with him.   She'll go shopping with him, to the movies with him, and he will be the first person she calls when she needs help moving to a new apartment.   She'll even invite him over to watch something on cable. She might even snuggle with him. She'll be cool with him until he tries to get romantic. At that point she'll use her foot to stomp him back into the friend zone he tried to escape from. He's a nice guy though, he'll hang in there because he feels like his kindness will win her over.

The third man is the Oral Guy. This dude is on the roster because he got a good tongue. This the guy who will eat the poo, lick that clit, and some will even get that tongue up in the booty hole. Some women will let the Oral Guy suck on their breasts and nothing else. The thing about the Oral Guy is that she will not reciprocate by sucking his dick. She sure as hell won't let him stick his penis in her vagina. The Oral Guy is the type who is cool with just eating the poo because he is happy a woman is giving him some form of sex. If the woman is on her game she may hold out the promise of going ass-up for him. Not going to happen but she'll still dangle the carrot in front of him.

The fourth guy is the Public Guy. This is the man she'll go on public dates with and slide him the tongue at the end of the night. After a few dates she'll even sleep with him. The Public Guy is the one who is acceptable to family and friends. He's the one a woman will take to family gatherings and other than Uncle Junior making fun of him because he seems stiff he is accepted by her peoples. Sex with the Public Guy is standard. Not bad but not bed shattering. Public Guy won't make her get rid of Oral Guy because he isn't good at eating the poo. Public Guy is good boyfriend and maybe husband material.

The fifth guy is the Good-Good Man. This is the one she will have buck wild sex with. This the one who give her multiple orgasms. Good-Good Man got her ass up, legs up, up against the wall, on the kitchen floor, levitating in the living room, speaking in tongues, making contact with a distant galaxy, having a past life regression, and seeing the Great Pumpkin. A woman will act conservative around Oral Guy and Public Guy. She'll deep throat Good-Good Man. Nobody knows about Good-Good Man. They're not friends on social media. She doesn't tell her girlfriends about him because she knows those treacherous heifers will try to get at him. Thing is she chose Good-Good Man. She nervously approached him when he was at a club happy hour eating some buffalo wings. This is the one man she doesn't try to game because he wouldn't go for it anyway. She knows she shares him with other women but she doesn't care as he leaves her blissed out every single time.

Yeah it's a woman's game. The best game for a man to learn is not how to approach several woman but how to avoid getting played. Women learn the game from time they were babies when they discovered that daddy would come a running whenever they cried. They also paid attention to how their mothers lied to their daddies when the mother wanted to see their side pieces. A woman's level of game is incredible. Any man who wants to improve with women needs to get friendly with some honest women. Trust me, it would be worth the effort.

Why Smart Women Get Played

Now I wrote that women control the game but that's not an absolute. There are definitely times when women get played, dogged, ran through. Of course we will hear about how men dogged some poor innocent woman. Of course the narrative conveniently leaves out that the women who got "dogged" knowingly slept with a married man. She knew because the man's wife introduced them. Thing is she didn't get played because the man was a cheating bastard. The woman didn't get played because she was a backstabbing hoe. The woman got played because of her ego.

As I have mentioned I have talked to thousands of women. I've heard everything so I definitely heard different women tell me how they got dogged by some man or in many cases men. The women will come up with everything from that the man was a psychopath to that he hated his mother.

I would listen to the women and nod and "um hmm" at appropriate places. I may have talked with thousands of women but I definitely wasn't friends with the overwhelming majority of them. Now for the friends I would tell them what I really thought. Women who know me well know I can be very direct, even crude in my responses to a relationship question. It was tough love and I've had more than one woman thank me for being honest. One way or the other I told these women the same thing. I will share that now.

The reason women get played is not because they lack common sense, love thugs, or have a sign on their foreheads that says, "Victim." The reason women get played is because of their egos. The women who get played the most are the ones who think they are the bomb. Even though all women can and do get played there is one type that gets played the most. I will call that woman the Smart Woman. The Smart Woman is usually educated. If she isn't educated she may have had enough intelligence to work her way up to a high paying job. The Smart Woman has money. She has a home and material goods. As far as physical appearance she will be somewhere between decent looking to slightly above average. She's definitely not ugly but no one will mistake her for a Dime. From most men's point of view the Smart Woman will be considered girlfriend or wife material. Now here's where it gets interesting. I said "most men's point of view." The men who will indeed have a high regard for the Smart

Woman will be the same men that most women see as Non-Select.

As I said Smart Women think they are the bomb. Non-Select men agree with them. The Good Guys who are realistic see these women as perfect compliments. No these women aren't Dimes but to the Good Guys who like them, they are. They want a good moral woman to come home to and that's what the Smart Woman looks like. Many Good Guys want to build with these women. The problem is that the Good Guys aren't good enough for the Smart Woman. Smart Women don't see good men they can build a family with. Smart Women see men who are too short, too slim, too fat, and not handsome enough. They don't see a man who has worked hard to get where he is. They see a man who is not making enough money, who may not have finished college, who is blue collar, and who lives in a modest apartment instead of a big townhouse. The Good Guys don't have what the Smart Women want.

The Smart Women want Mr. Goodbar and the Masked Man. They want the man who can make them scream. It's more than that though. They want the top men period. Women are very competitive with each other. They want the man that other women want. They want to be able to say they got **THE ONE!** This is a key aspect of a woman's game. Some women are realistic enough to be happy for what they can actually get. Dude may be short and pudgy but he loves them and will always do right by them. That ain't good enough for the Smart Woman. She wants that tall, handsome, built, man with degrees and money. Some will even reject Goodbar if he isn't classically handsome or broke.   Here's the funny thing.   In my opinion there's nothing wrong with a woman going for the top man.   Go for it girl! Get yo man!   The problem that pops up is that the top men don't see the Smart Women in the same light.

There was a Masked Man I knew years ago.   He said something that summed up what I heard other Masked Men say over the years in one way or the other.   He mocked Smart Women by saying, "I'm educated. I have a house and car. I keep my hair fixed and wear nice clothes. I'm 250 lbs. I can't figure out why men don't want me."   Men in general don't care about woman's accomplishments and material possessions.   The few that do usually do so because they may be in a social circle where being with a person who projects a certain image is important. Usually in upper middle class social groups. In general that shit don't matter or is at least not the first thing men notice.   When men talk with other men about a woman they just met they don't talk about her degree, her profession, or her big house. They say she pretty with a phat ass.   To Select Men most Smart Women are average at best. When a man doesn't see a woman as a Dime he will not give her his best. This is especially the case if he has numerous women to choose from.   Each sub category of the Select will respond to Smart Women in interesting ways.

Mr. Goodbar sees most women as sex partners.   For the most part the Goodbars are the ones stroking the Dimes.

Smart Women usually don't appear on a Goodbar's radar. When they do the Smart Woman is usually nothing more than physical gratification. Even then she probably had to work hard and spend money to get Goodbar's attention. At some point the Smart Woman's emotions become involved and she falls in love with Goodbar. Goodbar on the other hand just likes her doggy style. At some point the Smart Woman becomes a burden and Goodbar moves on. He usually has other women anyway. Now of course the Smart Woman feels that Goodbar took advantage of her. She forgets that she chased him and not the other way around. She really played herself.

Now the Masked Man is a completely different story. A Goodbar may not set out to intentionally dog a woman. The Masked Man may make it his life mission to do so. Now this isn't all Masked Men yet there a sizable number who will intentionally hurt a woman emotionally. The Masked Man didn't start out as Select. He had to work to get there. Physically he had to hit the gym hard. He had to build his body, he had to work on his grooming, his dental work, and his clothing style. That's just the physical piece. He also had to go through college and maybe graduate school. For the few blue collar Masked Men they had to put in long hours to learn and master their craft. The Masked Man had to pay some dues. The issue is that while they were paying their dues they had very little female companionship. When these men were Non-Select they got rejected for numerous reasons. I knew this dude who eventually became a high paid attorney. He said while he was in school women rejected him because he didn't have money to spend on them. Never mind he was in school to become an attorney. I've heard plenty of stories like that. The irony is that once many of these men started making money the same women that rejected them would get real friendly saying something like, "I knew you were going places. I always thought you were fine." Really? What happens is the Masked Man has had years to build up some resentment. There's another dynamic with this.

When the Masked Man was just a Good Guy he wanted the Smart Woman. She just didn't want him back. Once he crosses the boundary into the Select World that Smart Woman doesn't look as good to him anymore. This is even in situations where her physical appearance hasn't faded. The Masked Man got his money right, his house and car are big, his body is muscular, and he can wear expensive tailor made suits. Dude wants a Dime to complete the picture. He'll be cool as long as he dealing with a Dime. When he deals with a Smart Woman he will treat her in an inferior way. All this pain and frustration he has carried for years will be taken out on a Smart Woman even though she may genuinely be attracted to him.

Years ago I did a radio show where I talked specifically about men who dog women. I told the beautiful host that the biggest and most dangerous dogs are not trying to talk to women in the streets. The biggest dogs aren't some men with their pants hanging off their ass. The most doggish men, the ones who make it their life mission to hurt women, are often the ones who are professionals with corporate jobs.   It's all part of a vicious cycle.   Smart Women think they should get the top men and reject men who aren't there. When those men get to the top they reject those same women that rejected them.

I had to speak on this.   I've heard so many women complain about not finding a good man but it's always their egos that get in the way.   A woman can have five Good Guys chasing her but because she thinks she's the woman she wants Mr. Goodbar or the Masked Man. Then she will have the nerve to complain that there is a "shortage of good man." She get out her ego and humble herself she will see that there are several men for her to choose from.   Her ego though makes her chase that man who may dog her.   Many men are told to stay in their lanes when looking for mates.   That good piece of advice works both ways.

The Sexual Shadow World

Many men on the internet call themselves Red Pill. They seriously believe they have discovered something about male/female interactions that has made them more enlightened than the rest of the population. Maybe they do have a little bit more knowledge than men in their peer group but really they are at the tip of the iceberg. They really don't know how deep the rabbit hole goes. How could they? It's one thing to think you have knowledge of something. It's another thing to directly experience something. When people have experienced certain things it's easy to recognize by people who have experienced the same thing. One experience that I can tell many so-called Red Pillers have not had is the Sexual Shadow World.

The Sexual Shadow World (Shadow World) is not a physical place. It is a shadow. A shadow out of the corner of one's eyes.   It is the realm where a few men and a whole lot of women express their sexuality free from society's constraints.   It is where the stay at home soccer mom who makes the nice cupcakes for the neighborhood families has had an ongoing relationship with her young hot neighbor for years.   It is where the high functioning autistic but good looking man who works in a library supplements his income by indulging in the fantasies of lonely but affluent women. It's a world that occasionally leaks out into the mainstream but remains quite hidden.   Someone introduced to this world would have their minds blown.

To be clear, the Swinger and BDSM subcultures are not really a part of the Shadow World.   There are clubs and other public venues that cater to these subcultures.   No the Shadow World is something that caters primarily to the lustful cravings of sexually frustrated women.   Indeed it was created and maintained by women.

I've already discussed a woman's sexual nature and that many women have several men.   The issue is that as a result of the social mores in most cultures on the planet women have not been as free to pursue their sexual desires. Things are changing of course, but there is still a stigma against women being sexually free.   Their vaginas, however, refused to be denied.   They are going to get theirs.   Hence the Shadow World.

In the Shadow World women do not invite men according to how much money they make.   They do not care about a man's status.   Most social considerations are nonexistent in the Shadow World. Only thing that matters is raw unbridled lust. They don't care about a man's race or age. If he looks good which in the Shadow World means he looks fuckable he is invited into that special place. The key to a man becoming a part of the Shadow World is his sex appeal. I'm going to go deeper into that subject.

I've already talked about looks being important to women. For a man to get into the Shadow World it takes more. Many people mistakenly believe that good looks automatically equals sex appeal. It doesn't. A person can be physically attractive with a facial structure and body build that is found pleasing to look at by a wide variety of people. Models make money because of their pleasing physical features. Yet few people use the term sexy to describe models. Their beauty typically doesn't make the average dick hard or vagina tingle. They still look good though. Just not erotic.

Contrast models with pornstars. Pornstars tend to have comparable physical features to models but beautiful or handsome are not the first words that come to mind when people see them. People will say pornstars are "hot," "sexy," and "fuckable." The pornstars have the looks but they also have something extra that puts them at another level of sexual desirability.

One could say that there are two types of beauty. There is artistic beauty and erotic beauty. Artistic beauty is good to look at and be admired. Erotic beauty stimulates one's loins. I first noticed this many years ago with two

51

sisters I knew. They were both very physically attractive. The first sister more so from an artistic point of view. On her face and figure alone men would probably rate her a 9.5. She was good to look at and men chased her as a result but they would get turned off once they got to know her. She was far from mean though, very pleasant to get along with, but she wasn't a woman who enhanced her femininity. She wore very little makeup and never wore clothes that showed her figure as her clothing style was dull. The second sister on the other hand, would probably be rated an 8 by men but she had no problem wearing tight clothes, makeup, and heels. Plus she had a very seductive stare she gave men. Her beauty came off as more erotic.

So there are two levels of sex appeal. Being considered good looking is the first level. It will draw a person's attention but may not seal the deal. At that point it is mostly about personality compatibility. This is the level Red Pillers are familiar with. Most will agree the being good looking is very important. A person can reach that level and still have issues. The thing is that they will only be attractive to a finite amount of people. Beauty is in the eye of the beholder. A man may be tall and muscular with a square jaw and piercing eyes and there will still be women who find him unattractive. Their preference may be a regular size man with a round face and stockier build. A person's physical preferences are influenced by their race, culture, and bloodlines. There is no such thing as a universal beauty standard. Women especially will reject men who do not meet their personal criteria. Now that was level one.

Level Two is a sex appeal that goes across racial, cultural, and bloodline boundaries. It is a primal attraction that is intangible in nature. It is a masculine energy that is present in a man, a lion, or a termite. It is a feminine energy that is present in a woman, a cat, and a spider. It's a deep energy that people cannot perceive consciously but know it when they feel it. A man radiating that type of energy will be felt by any woman and sometimes gay man in the vicinity. A woman radiating that primal feminine energy will be felt by every man and sometimes lesbian in the vicinity. I talk about how to develop that energy in all of my non-fiction books so I won't go over it here. I gave that brief presentation in order to provide a context for the type of men who are invited into the Shadow World. The common denominator for men in the Shadow World is that they are operating at Level Two.

Women in their secret worlds are not looking for protectors and providers. Many of them have that already. Many women have what many call an Alpha Male. I'll give my thoughts on that Alpha Male thing in a later section. Many women in the Shadow World have a tall, handsome man with money. Only problem is the sex life isn't fulfilling. The problem is typically a combination of a man lacking sex skills and a woman who stays with the man because of other considerations. She may even love him in a way. The sole purpose of the men in the Shadow World is to give her good orgasms. This is a major consideration when women choose men for this world. Here's where it gets interesting. The men chosen for this world goes against not only conventional wisdom but the ideas of those who think they've taken the Red Pill.

The men in this world are typically the men I identify as Goodbars. The men are typically handsome but most probably couldn't make money as models. They have above average body builds but only a few would get their pictures shared on social media. They tend not to have money and status. What they have is an erotic aura which draws women to them like a magnet. The stories these men have told me over the years. For that matter the stories that women who have slept with these men have told me over the years.

Many men think they have game. They have different strategies for approaching, dating, and sexing women. The men in the Shadow World flip that game on its head. These men are **CONSISTENTLY** approached by women on the streets, on jobs, in malls, and at grocery stores. This a game that Goodbar types learn to play at a young age.

One important consideration I need to mention about the men in the Shadow World is that they tend to be discreet. Many men lie on their dicks by inflating the number of women they've slept with. Some will even lie and say they slept with a particular woman. Men who have truly been in the Shadow World never talk about the women they've been with unless they are around another man who has been in the Shadow World. When a woman chooses a man based off of pure lust one thing she thinks about is if this dude who she wants to go ass-up for is going to talk. After all she's married to the pastor of a church. One time I was talking with a married woman, just shooting the breeze. We got on the subject of cheating mates. I said I was the type who keeps his lips sealed. She looked me dead in the eye and with a serious tone said, "You're the type of man I would cheat with." So when a woman chooses a man for the Shadow World she is not only looking for a hot fuckable body but she's also looking for someone who can keep his mouth shut.

I know many men are reading this and wondering how to get into the Shadow World since looks, money, status, or game won't get them there. The clues are my first book *Nice Guys and Players*. It was written from a Shadow World perspective.

Understanding Sex Appeal

I guarantee some men, and maybe a few women, have read the last section and thought I was wack. For so many people looks and sex appeal are the same thing. So that there is no confusion I'm going to break things down even further so that even the densest bamma can understand. For those who don't know, "bamma" is slang used in the Washington, DC area. Calling someone a bamma is similar to calling them a lame. Now you bammas know. Women, for the most part know what I'm talking about because they learn from childhood how to cultivate their sex appeal. Some better than others of course. Let me give you a visual.

You have a woman we'll call Linda. Linda has a great looking face. She has soft skin, with big eyes, a small nose and full luscious lips. She also has high cheekbones and long hair that goes halfway down her back. She has a long elegant neck, soft shoulders, with round perky breasts, a small waist which expands to curvy hips and a perfectly round booty. On top of that she has long shapely legs. Based on the description alone she should be considered very sexy and alluring. She barely registers on the radar of most men. Now why is this? According to conventional wisdom and dubious academic studies she should be a highly desirable woman who oozes sex appeal. Let's add some more elements to the description.

The first thing to consider about Linda is that she may physically look like a fashion model with an optimal face and body but in reality she is very masculine. Though she has long hair she never styles it and she wears it in the same manner as a long haired man. Linda never wears makeup or feminine earrings. The clothes she wears are men's clothes. Wearing heels are out of the question. She even walks like a man. If she is sexually appealing to anyone it is femme lesbians. At best most men see her as one of the guys. Some even think she is a man who looks like a girl. Farfetched scenario? Not hardly.

I've read several blogs, studies, and watched several videos of those who promote the concept that looks matter. Of course I agree as improving one's body has been the foundation of my books. That being said there's another level. If you look at the information in the public sphere it gives the impression that **ALL** one needs to do is look good. Many people feel like if they get some type of plastic surgery then their relationship issues will disappear. They may get a little bit more attention but if other things are not in place that person will not be considered "sexy."

Even though we all have different ideas of what is considered sexy there are also some commonalities. The foundation of sex appeal is the body. Not the face as some people may think though there are men and women who are described as having sexy faces. An honest assessment of the people outside of celebrities who are considered sexy will show that these men and women tend to have average looking faces at best. What they have is other things that make them sexually appealing. The first is the body. The second thing is their masculine or feminine energy. If the word "energy" is too New Age for some folks let's use the term "mannerisms." A sexy man will behave in a distinctly masculine manner. A sexy woman will behave in a distinctly feminine manner. Their behaviors will match their physical appearance. Women especially know what I'm talking about. Many have met a man they thought to be very good looking but got turned off when the man started acting and talking in a feminine manner. So we have the body and behavior that matches the physical appearance of that body. There are still more ingredients.

Instead of saying looks are important it may be accurate to say "the look" is important. Sexy men and women will dress and adorn themselves in a manner which will draw the attention of the opposite sex to their bodies. Women are especially adept at this. A sexy woman will wear heels, silk stockings, a mini skirt, and a low cut top that shows off her breasts. Men will tend to wear fitted shirts and tailored suits when dressed up. When dressed casual, sexy men will wear tight T-shirts which will show off their chest and arms. Some men will wear pants that will show their dick prints. Sexy people will wear clothing that will draw attention to them in a sexual way. Now some people may wear bright colors or eccentric looking clothing. They are drawing attention to themselves in an artistic way but they are probably not turning anyone on sexually. The overwhelming majority of people dress in a way to deflect attention away from themselves. They dress in a manner which does not show off their bodies.

Another factor is how sexy people engage other people. Sexy people flirt with folks. They don't have dry conversations or ask indirect questions. A sexy person knows how turn someone on with their words. This is very important. A man can have a great body, have masculine mannerisms, and wear clothes that draw women to his big chest and muscular arms. Of course he draws women to him. He still loses out if he does not have a flirty conversation. Example time again.

You have a man named Larry. Larry is tall with a big chest and big arms. He has a very manly posture and dresses in way that draws the attention of the ladies. Women will approach him and after talking with Larry a while they get turned off. Now in many cases a woman gets turned off if a good looking man sounds or acts stupid. This isn't Larry's problem. The issue is that he is too serious. His conversation is boring and dry. He speaks in a slow monotone. Larry doesn't know how to flirt. Whatever initial sex appeal Larry had is killed because he doesn't know how to engage a woman in a sexual manner. A woman may still deal with him because of his body but it will likely be a brief affair at best. Most women will be turned off.

I've mentioned this before and it bears repeating. For a person to be considered sexy another person has to look at them and want to have sex. That's the very definition of sexy. Everybody is sexually appealing to **SOMEBODY**. People with sex appeal are people who draw the **SEXUAL** attention of a significant number of other people. When other people see them they don't think, "This person would make a good buddy." They don't think, "This person is probably a smart intelligent person who will go far in life." People look at a truly sexy person and think, "They can get it."

Looks by itself doesn't make a person sexy. Money and status sure as hell don't make a person sexy, particular men. Many women think they are catches because they have degrees and six figure salaries. Sorry Charlene, that's not the case. That thing call game definitely doesn't make a man sexy. The key to sex appeal is the intangibles. It's the proper gender dynamic, the confidence to wear certain types of clothing, and the ability to engage another person in a sexual manner.

Pretty Boy Problems

Despite what I wrote in the previous section looks still matter. Don't get it twisted. Yes people can have more sex appeal than looks but a good looking man or woman will always get play. I've said it throughout this book and most people with an even smidgen of common sense knows this even if they don't want to admit it publically. There's something about this notion that no talks about. I haven't heard it directly articulated publically or privately. The thing I'm talking is that yes looks matter but not necessarily **GOOD** looks. Focusing this conversation on what women like to look at in men, they don't always lust over men most people would consider good looking. Let me share another story with you.

The most interesting and direct rejection I received in life was based on my looks. This woman told me the exact reason why she wasn't going to have sex with me. She wasn't mean about it and quite frankly I took the rejection as a compliment. We were talking on the phone and she said to me, "Rom I couldn't date you because you're too pretty." "Too pretty?" I asked her. I was surprised she said that. Despite how confident or arrogant I can come off sometimes my confidence is based on intangible factors such as my ability to stay calm amid chaos. Plus many women have liked my overall style. I really don't think much of my facial features and I describe myself as average looking. I mean women have always said they liked my eyes but I attributed that to my uncle teaching me to always look people in the eye. Many women have complimented my body especially when I worked out like crazy but I didn't think "pretty." This young lady said I was "too pretty" because of my eyes and my skin. She got hot over rough looking men. I just laughed because I rarely took rejection personally especially over something I had no control over. It was a good lesson though. Sometimes a man can look too good to a woman.

In my life I have a met a few men who women considered physically attractive above and beyond the rest of the male population. Even other men would look at these guys and say the dudes looked good. Now conventional wisdom would suggest that these men made out like bandits with women. Anybody looking at them would assume they had harems. Naw. The pretty boys I've met in my life have either been very monogamous or very single. Yes they had a whole bunch of women lusting after them, in some case even butch lesbians.   Lusting after someone is one thing. Actually having sex with that person is another.   One thing with Pretty Boys is that they will have trouble because many women are intimidated by them.

Many women are very insecure.   They can strut around like Amazons ready to conquer the world and whatnot. They can make a business deal in the morning and then go home to their big expensive houses and whip up a fabulous dinner for themselves to eat while they watch their big screen TVs.   Yeah many women are dripping strength and confidence until they meet that drop dead gorgeous man who's tall and buffed. That same woman who just addressed executives at a board meeting has trouble saying hello to the man as he walks by.   If she does speak she'll stutter and once he walks by she'll rush home to change her panties because she peed on herself.   It's not that women don't want Pretty Boys.   It's just that the butterflies are doing the tango in their stomachs.   Just like men get anxiety around beautiful women, women get it worse around beautiful men.

Even in situations where a Pretty Boy will take the initiative and approach a woman there are still problems. Even the most beautiful of women really don't think they're beautiful.   Some will even think they are ugly.   So when a Pretty Boy approaches them the first thing they are thinking is, "Why is this fine man approaching me?"   A woman will assess that man's looks and assume that he already has ten girlfriends.   Some women will even reject this man because despite his looks they don't want to be a part of a harem. This is just one scenario.

Another situation I've observed a lot is when a Pretty Boy is in a social group where women have time to check him out. Now they'll ask about him and may even be in a position to talk to him. They already see he is handsome. They talk to him and find out he is also very intelligent and also has a cool personality. It comes out that the man is single and doesn't date a lot. What women will do in this situation is start asking, "What's wrong with him?" In a woman's mind a fine man should always have a woman or at least some prospects. They may start asking questions to see what's wrong with him. Something will always be wrong because the dude may look good but he is still human. Some women magnify a small fault into something major. Then there's the one stigma Pretty Boys have to deal not only from women but from men as well. People will wonder if he is gay.

I've heard women just straight up call a very handsome man gay even if he doesn't show any signs of being a homosexual. Some women even look for it because they are looking for some flaw. This stems from their own insecurity. Men on the other hand are just jealous because this Pretty Boy is typically getting more attention than they are. Many men have a bad habit of putting another man down in front of women. Brotherhood goes out the door when a pretty face, big tits, and a phat ass are involved.

A Pretty Boy will have trouble with women because it takes a while for women to get comfortable around them. For that reason Pretty Boys tend to be monogamous. They tend to either get with an equally beautiful woman or the more average woman that had a chance to click with the personality of a Pretty Boy.

It's because of the problems that the Pretty Boys face that the men who legitimately have high sex counts tend not to be drop dead good looking. An honest look at the men who get a lot of sex the most common denominator is a better than average body build. These men, the Goodbars, will be considered handsome but it's not a raw bone structure type of handsome. I thought so at first and said as much in my first book. One thing about me though is that I will change my stance on something when presented with a better perspective. I wrote *Nice Guys and Players*, back in the late nineties. Since that time I have met and interacted with several high sex count men. These men would be considered above average handsome but their looks were more the result of a conscious cultivation as opposed to winning the genetic lottery. The Goodbars made themselves more handsome. Still, it was the type of handsome that women felt comfortable with. Let me share some wisdom I wrote about in *Nice Guys and Players*.

In *Nice Guys and Players*, I mentioned I learned a lot from a buddy I called Jim. I never forget what Jim told me about why beautiful women would always like me. He said, "Rom, beautiful women will always like you because you don't look better than they do." That was some powerful wisdom and the reason I never considered myself any more than decent looking. Beautiful women loved my ass to death. I've had homely women who would try to play me while model pretty and stripper sexy women would blow up my phone. Why knock what worked? The key with me though was that beautiful women were comfortable enough around me not to be intimidated.

One may wonder why I'm talking about Pretty Boys. It's not really about the Pretty Boys. The issue is more about men who feel like their genetics work against them. Many men who know that looks matter feel like they are not handsome enough or tall enough to attract beautiful women. Something that is not talked about enough publically is that there is a growing industry for male beauty products and also plastic surgery. I'm not going to knock it but I will say this. Every single man is a Mr. Goodbar to some woman. The facial features that some women may consider ugly on one man are considered beautiful by other women. I've met some very beautiful women who stated a preference for men under 6 feet tall. I've seen them with the men and I can tell when a woman is really feeling a man. Even with body builds all women don't want a muscular man. It's not a case of them settling. Some women prefer slim men. A few like fat men. Many, many women like a man who is somewhere between muscular and fat. Women will say, "Damn he thick!" I know a very beautiful woman who's so sexy that I've seen her put men into trances. One dude made up a poem about her on the spot. She would only mess with men she called ugly. She popped out three kids for her ugly husband.

Now someone may say this invalidates the notion that looks matter. Not at all. A woman **SEES** that a man is short, slim, thick, decent looking or ugly. She is still making a determination based on **LOOKS**.

For the men reading this work on what you have. Don't worry about the Pretty Boys as they got their own issues.

The Real Deal with Alpha Males

There is the thought that women want Alpha Males. It's something that I've promoted myself on occasion. The Alpha Male is supposedly that tall, handsome man with a take charge dominant personality. He kicks ass in all areas of society. He's the CEO of the billion dollar corporation, the football quarterback, the charismatic leader of the drug cartel. He is… **THE MAN.** The wisdom is that these men get the best women. Indeed it is thought these men will have harems of beautiful women who are at their beck and call. Most dating and seduction advice geared towards men provide techniques for a man to either become an Alpha Male or to imitate alpha characteristics. Too bad it's all bullshit.

To be clear there are men out there who are hitting on all cylinders like that. These men are tall, handsome, and smart. These men are superior athletes and have above average intelligence. They also have a healthy combination of street smarts and book smarts. These men will be wildly successful in whatever endeavors they choose to pursue. These men are also extremely rare. I've met thousands of people in my life. That being said, I can count the number of these rare men on two hands. I actually did that one time and got to the second hand in like three days. It was something I had to think hard about. These men are damn near urban legends. Women who stay single until they find one of these men should start looking for good veterinarians because their futures will include a lot of cats. The few such men I've met on this level only dealt with women who rated at least a 9 on the infamous scale. The ugliest woman I've seen with one of these men with was like an 8.5. While her "face" was 8.5 her sex appeal was 13. The average man is not going to have the genetics to be one of these men even with plastic surgery and working out.

Now men who are **PHYSICALLY** Alpha Males are more common. They are seen all over the place. The only thing is that for most part they don't have the mental traits of so-called Alpha Males. These men aren't confident. Many are more likely to be flunkies as opposed to leaders. Many such men are boy toys for ugly women with money. Economically many of these men work on low paying jobs. A significant portion of these men live criminal lifestyles and will at some point get caught into the prison system. Thus the notion that women prefer thugs over decent men. Naw it's just that many thugs also have nice bodies.

Here's a reality. Women will constantly talk about the personality traits they want in a man. It's the traits of the so-called Alpha Male. In men, women want confidence, competence, leadership, protectiveness, and the ability to provide. There are millions of men out there who have these traits. Ironically these men are the ones most likely to be single. Even when these men aren't single they tend to have less than ideal relationships. According to the prevailing "wisdom" of dating and relationship experts these men should be making out like bandits. That's not the case.

When people are told about men who have trouble getting into relationships several negative assumptions are made. One assumption made is that these men are ugly basement dwelling losers with poor social skills. There's some truth there but only a tiny percentage of single men fit this profile. Most single men are hardworking men who have steady jobs and have homes and working automobiles. These men are more than self-sufficient.

One interesting assumption is that these men are blue-collar guys and as such are not attractive to increasing numbers of college educated women. That's some bullshit. An honest look at the population of single men will reveal a large number of college graduates. This is something I can attest to from personal experience. I've done a lot of workshops, seminars, and relationship discussion panels. The men in the audience were not blue collar guys or members of the lumpen proletariat. I've done many a seminar with men who were at a minimum college graduates.

I sat on a panel one time with Ph.D.'s who complained that they were single but looking. Just to be clear many of the educated men I encountered were actively looking for women to connect with romantically. If one listens to the women looking for college graduates these men should have had full date calendars. We know that this is not the case.

These men are more than educated. These men are confident. They are smart. They are cool to be around. They can make women laugh. They can take charge. They are willing to provide for women. And for the women who say they want thugs for "protection," these men can fight too. Now here's the thing. I'm not the one saying all of this about the men. The most important thing is what women are saying about these men. I've had women tell me a whole lot about the men in their lives. They have told me about the men they fuck and the men they keep as friends. Many, many, women who complain about being dogged by some pretty boy or sexy dude will talk about that one man who had all the personality traits they want in a man. The only thing missing was that **SPARK.** They will say that they didn't feel any sexual chemistry with an otherwise good man.

In my book, *Nice Guy and Players*, I made what was probably the most important and indeed most quoted statement:

Sex is really the major difference between a nice guy and a player.

71

Women have dual needs in a relationship. The nature of society, however, is that the average woman will not articulate her sexual needs publically. Indeed many will not talk about their needs even in private settings. What's deep is that there are women so sexually repressed that they are not even consciously aware of their true sexual needs. At least until a predatory Goodbar reads her and starts pushing some buttons.

Women publically say they want one thing but privately want something else. Yes publically they want the personality traits of an Alpha Male. Okay that's more than fair. Go for the best. The problem is that the men who have these traits are the most likely to be single. Even when these men do get into relationships they are likely dealing with women who are more attracted to their money and status. Many women will say they are looking for a doctor or a lawyer. Those are titles. It says nothing about the character or personalities of the men who hold those titles. If a lawyer is in a relationship with a woman who was looking for a lawyer how can he know she wants him for him? What happens when that lawyer decides he wants to be a landscaper? Many professionals leave their careers to pursue their passions. Will the woman who married a lawyer stick around for a landscaper? Probably not. You see where I'm going with this?

If a man is successful as a lawyer he will be successful as a landscaper. The personality traits needed to succeed in any endeavor are the generally the same. It all comes down to drive, will power, and intelligence. These are generally considered Alpha Male traits. If the woman was truly attracted to the traits it wouldn't matter what the man did for a living. There are many men who have that drive, will-power, and intelligence. The **ONLY** issue is that these traits seldom come in a physically enticing body.

The media got people's perceptions of what a superior man looks like fucked up. In the movies the action hero, the morally ambiguous crime boss, and the business executive all look like buffed pretty boys. Even if they play something like a biker they look like pretty boys. Even their tattoos and dirty clothes will be pretty. People, particularly women, see this and take it as reality. Here's something to think about. A person's subconscious takes in everything it encounters as real, particularly images. The subconscious doesn't make a distinction between reality and fantasy. On its own anyway. If someone sees a person flying on a movie screen it will be taken as fantasy **IF** they are critical at the moment they see the person fly. They need only think, "People can't fly" at that moment and the subconscious records the moment as fantasy. Most people don't do that. I remember when people were more into soap operas back in the day. Women, especially, would talk about the characters as if they were real people. That's a problem. That's a problem with romance novels. Many women subconsciously take them as real. This is no joke. I've met educated women who said they wanted a man similar to a character seen in a movie.   Many women are actually looking for a drop dead gorgeous billionaire who would fall in love with a Plain Jane.

The reality is that the men who kick the most ass in society are likely be short, or slim, or overweight. I've known a lot of men who have successfully built up viable business enterprises over the years.   They wouldn't be able to make money as models.   I've known several dozen men who have been in the military or Federal Agents.   Except for two of them who did look like they were out of central casting, these were ordinary looking fellows.   The real heroes are ordinary until circumstances force them to become more.   Those are the real Alpha Males.

Now many dating coaches and seduction gurus will suggest that if men would just imitate the behavior of these men beautiful women would just come a running.   Many men will do that.   They will develop confident body language and speech tone.   They will assert themselves to take charge in a situation.   Some women may even engage them in a public venue.   At the end of the night though that man doing everything he think is Alpha goes home to pull his dick.

Contrast that with a man I knew I'll call Kyle.   Kyle was soft spoken, and not very assertive.   Behavior wise he went against everything dating coaches preach.   Based on just his mannerisms he would be characterized as a sexually frustrated nice guy.   He probably had one of the highest AND quality sex counts I've ever seen with a man.   I've known several of his women.   They were all in the 7 – 8 range as far as looks and sex appeal.   Despite being quiet,

74

women found him to be very physically attractive. One woman told me he was "beautiful" and another said she wanted to "rape him." He was good guy but he didn't fit prevailing image of an Alpha Male as far as his personality.

As with everything else dealing with male/female relationships as a culture we need to examine many of our beliefs. They are not serving us. If women really wanted what are considered Alpha Males, many men would not be involuntarily single. There are all of these college educated women running around saying that there is a shortage of college educated men. If that is the only issue then **EVERY** single college educated man should have several women. We all know that this isn't the case.

The Great Dime Chase

Let's be real about something. The reason men are shelling out thousands of dollars to attend seminars, watch countless videos, and read blogs is to get beautiful women. Not beautiful on the inside either. Many men want the top notch woman, the ten on the infamous scale. They want the Dime. They don't want the women they can actually get who would probably love them, make ham sandwiches for them, and suck that dick in its entirety. That's because the woman who actually wants them is homely and 50 pounds overweight. Sometimes that woman comes with a bad attitude. To quote a mentor, that woman may be built like a water buffalo with the disposition of a wild gorilla. A man ain't trying to settle for that. They want the finest babe in the land. And they want to make sure all their peers know that.   There's problems with wanting that fine woman though.

One of the main problems is that there are not enough Dimes to go around.   A man may not want to deal with the woman built like a water buffalo but he may live in a town with a whole herd of them.   The only time a man may consistently see Dimes is when he lives near a big college town or if he hangs around the most popular club in a big city.   Even then many of the Dimes are just Nickels who shined themselves up real good.   It's interesting that there is so much talk about a shortage of good men yet it would be easy for men to say that there is a shortage of good women. Unlike women, men would be honest enough to say that we mean beautiful and sexy.

Before I really get into this I have a confession to make.   Unlike most other heterosexual men I don't get excited about beautiful or sexy women.   At least until I get to know them.   I can think of only three times I've looked at a Dime and lost my mind.   I managed to get over that though. One of my secret weapons with beautiful women is that I can remain calm around them.   Most men act stupid around Dimes.   If I want to see a man's character I bring him around a beautiful woman.   Trust me any personality strengths and flaws will come out.   This is especially the case when the Dime rejects a man.   I have never seen this to fail. Unless that man is someone like me.

The reason I don't get excited about beautiful women is that I have mostly Dimes in my immediate family.   Starting

77

with my maternal grandmother, she looked like she was in her thirties when she was in her sixties with smooth, almost blemish free skin. My mother worked as a paid model in the late fifties. My grandmother and mother talked about opening a modeling school. My mother actually taught me some modeling steps. My cousins are very attractive. I had one cousin that got street harassed so much she could give a seminar on how to handle the attention. Let's just say the women in my family had zero problems attracting men. What it did for me was get me used to being around beautiful women. Whereas for most men Dimes are goddesses to be put on pedestals for me they're people who mess up a brotha's comic book collection. Growing up around the women in my family allowed me to always get past a woman's beauty and look at her personality traits.

Even when I wrote *Nice Guys and Players* and *Sexual Chemistry* I only devoted a single chapter in each book to dealing with beautiful women. My feeling was that the average man would look for a decent looking woman and be cool with that. Boy was I wrong. I had one man buy *Sexual Chemistry* and he turned right to the chapter where I wrote about dealing with extremely attractive women. He didn't care about the rest of the book. He wanted what he wanted. That's cool though. Like I said there will be problems.

As I said there are not enough Dimes to go around. This creates competition between men. You have ten men going for the same woman. That woman has a tendency to develop an ego. I've seen this even with the best of them.

The Dimes who are generally good persons may not take advantage of men directly but she will not likely turn down gifts and other things from her "friends." The ones with the worst characters will tend to use men. Let's look at that further.

The power of the pussy is real. A naturally beautiful woman who successfully cultivates her sex appeal to its highest degree is a force of nature especially in a money driven materialistic society. A Dime can literally be born in a shack that doesn't even have an indoor toilet to an illiterate mother. Yet by the time that Dime is twenty she will be a millionaire. Men will do her bidding for the **PROMISE** of sex. She doesn't even have to have sex with most men. Most men are tricks to a degree. They don't have looks or what they think to be game so they approach a woman with their wallets in their hand. Many men think they can buy a woman even if she isn't a professional prostitute. They will take her on expensive dates, pay her bills, and do whatever she wants, before they even sniff the pussy. So imagine what many men do once the Dime "rewards" them with sex. That's real power. All these women thinking they are doing something working 60 hours a week around people who hate them have nothing on a Dime. All a Dime has to do is keep her gym membership up and good relations with her hairdresser and clothing shop clerks. The beauty is she doesn't have to pay for it. Men are competing to pay her bills.

The competition thing is deep because of the Select/Non-Select divide. When men call themselves "Good Men" and complain about women going for "Bad Boys" that's a competition over Dimes. Most women don't go for Bad Boys. Most Bad Boys don't go for every woman. The issue is that Good Men see Dimes with the Bad Boys. These Good Men have developed a false belief that since they have always done the right thing and they are good moral men they should be the ones who get the Dimes. That's all that is. If these Good Men really wanted women that appreciated them there are plenty of Plain Janes around who see these men as catches. The Good Men don't want the "Good Girls" though. They are chasing that Dime just like everybody else.

Many men would rather be single than deal with anything less than a Dime. This is unrealistic because these men are usually not A-1 themselves. Many men put beautiful women so high on a pedestal they forget that these women have their own preferences. One preference is that these Dimes want men who work out. To be clear this isn't about aesthetics though a Dime will go crazy over very handsome men. One observation I have made about beautiful and sexy women is that they will spend hours in a gym. Many Dimes played sports in high school and some in college. A woman who is into playing sports and staying in shape is not going to want a man who doesn't have the same interests. A woman looks for a man who reflects her inner values. If she values sports and fitness she will have an attraction for a man who values sports and fitness. Most

80

Goodbar types have played sports at some point in their lives especially the ones whose calling cards is their bodies.

Then you have some men who think they are going to "game" a Dime. I'm going write more in depth on game. Right now I'll say that game doesn't work with Dimes. The reason is that a beautiful and sexy woman has pretty much seen everything a man can throw at her since she hit puberty. For many even earlier when they had to dodge perverted uncles at family gatherings. Dimes will look at a man giving her a corny line and determine what she can get out of him. A man who thinks he "gamed" a Dime needs to make sure his credits cards are paid up. He will be using them a lot in the coming weeks. He might need a second job.

The only men who consistently pull Dimes without having to open their wallets are Goodbars. Dimes will approach Goodbars. I've even seen some Dimes get nervous around a Goodbar. Goodbar's secret? He isn't pressed about a Dime. Yeah she's fine but so were the other eight women who tried to get his attention. A dynamic with this is that a Dime is so used to men chasing her that the one man who doesn't chase her will seem intriguing. She will want to know what's up with this man. Especially if she can't pin his disinterest on him being gay. A Dime may even offer this man sex because his act of ignoring her actually turns her on.

There is so much that be said about the Dime chasing thing but I think the reader gets the gist. It's all about that beautiful and sexy woman. Many men are not happy until they acquire that woman. The thing is since Dimes are a relatively small population many men will live frustrated lives because they will never get a Dime.

The Best Women for Nerdy Guys

Let's keep it raw, many of the men who will read this book are the Geeks, Dorks, Lames, Nerds, and my favorite, Bammas. Collectively they I will refer to them as Nerdy Guys. Not all of course. Many Goodbars, Masked Men, and Gamesmen will read this book along with Average Joes. Many women will read this joint. Different people are going to get different things from this book. I know many Nerdy Guys are going to be looking for tips on how to get women. They are the main customers in the male dating advice industry. That's cool. I know many have read through this book and are wondering when I'm going to say anything useful since I guarantee much of what I'm saying is over their heads. I've decided to throw them a bone. First let me really define who I mean by Nerdy Guys beyond the few titles at the start of this paragraph.

People have different definitions of the word "Nerd." Generally all the definitions point to a man who is not seen as socially popular. He typically isn't the most handsome man or the most stylist dresser. On a real serious note the Nerdy Guy may show signs of being on the autism spectrum. I won't get too much into that. I personally define the Nerdy Guy as that person who doesn't socially fit into the crowd. He tends to be...off as far as his mannerisms and how he interacts with other people. He isn't the life of the party. As far as my four categories of men he would definitely fit into the Nice Guy category. Keep in mind, however, all Nice Guys are not Nerds. There are a lot of Average Joes who fit in socially with most people who are also in the Nice Guy category. There are several sub-categories within each group. Nerdy Guys are simply one subset of Nice Guys.

The interesting thing about many Nerds is that despite them not being the most handsome or popular or socially adept dudes many want the top notch women, the Dimes. Unless these Nerds also have big bank accounts that's not going to happen. One thing with many women is that as a group they tend to want men that other women want. Nerds are very seldom that man. Sorry Charlie. You gets nowhere near those lace thongs worn by the Dimes. The Dime will not look at the Nerd and start taking off her panties thinking, "I won't be needing these." Nope, no way, nada. Only in the movies and TV sitcoms.

Before some Nerdy Guy tries to figure out a way to hack into one of my online accounts I would like to point out that there is still hope for an attractive woman. Maybe not a Dime but someone who is feeling their gamer ass. Before I go there let's look at other general groups of women out there as far as their reaction to Nerdy Guys.

I talked about the Dimes in the last section. For the most part they are looking for a pretty boy, muscleman, or man with lots and lots of money. For those looking for money they are also looking for a man living a more glamorous lifestyle. Dimes are about looking good and being with men that look good. Dating coaches that sell the dream that a Nerdy Guy can get a Dime are either scammers or clueless as to a Dime's nature. Even at times when Nerds seem to be the in thing the image promoted is typically a male model wearing glasses or a pro ball player wearing hipster clothes. The models and pro athletes are still select. They can wear potato sacks and women will think they are sexy. So Dimes are out.

Next are the average everyday women. They are out too. Why? They are not Dimes but they follow the lead of Dimes. If Dimes aren't checking for Nerds, neither are the average women. It's like in high school where the most popular group of Dimes decide which group of boys will get the most attention. Once the Dimes set the tone, the other girls follow. Also the thing about average women is that they want to be the Dimes. The beauty industry is a multi-billion dollar industry for a reason. A Plain Jane will fix her hair, get

85

the make-up done at a department store cosmetics counter, and get the nails done. She will also get those 4 inch heels, lingerie from a specialty shop as well as body shaping wear. Finally she will get a tight dress and some silk stockings. She's not doing all that to hang out with a man she sees as a Nerdy Guy. She's hoping to catch a rich handsome man. She's living in fantasy world but it's her world. It doesn't include the socially awkward dude. Next.

I know, I just know some Nerdy Guys think I'm going to suggest they go after ugly women. Just to be clear I include not just facially unappealing women but women who are overweight in an unflattering way. A woman can be technically overweight but still shapely. I'm talking about the ones who don't have a shape. An ugly woman is simply physically unattractive which in this day and age is a problem. Cosmetics can be acquired from a corner drug store and anybody can walk around the block a few times for exercise. A woman being physically unattractive means there are deeper issues within her which must be addressed because even a smile can make any woman look better.

I strongly advise Nerdy Guys to stay away from ugly women. A problem is that many men, including Nerdy Guys, think ugly women are easy because well, they're ugly. Naw, they can be some of the hardest women to deal with. Ugly women get hit on probably more than Dimes. A man may be scared of being rejected by a Dime but will not give a fuck about approaching an ugly woman. Even if she rejects him he's not going to lose sleep. He'll just have a funny story for his boys. The woman may be ugly but she's not stupid. Some of the best female players I have met in life have been ugly women. A smart one will get something from a man trying to have sex with her. She may also have several men on her roster. A Nerdy Guy can get played by an ugly woman. Indeed even if she engages him she may still take out her frustrations with Mr. Goodbar on the Nerdy Guy.

Another issue is that despite being ugly, she too wants to be the Dime. She wants that lifestyle too. She wants to be seen with the rich handsome man pushing the E-Class Mercedes. She doesn't fantasize about the dorky guy who looks goofy and can't dress. Once again the Nerdy Guy is kicked to the curb. So what's left? Let me give you some "game" which the way I use it means knowledge. I'll start with a story.

I have a box at my local comic book store. I get three or four books a month and plus my sons have their section of the store they like. I noticed one interesting thing whenever I go there. There is always an attractive woman or young girl there. They might not be Dimes but the women typically range in the six to seven range on a scale of ten. Too many Nerdy Guys are so busy chasing Dimes they don't see their female equivalent, the Awkward Girls. By Awkward I mean these women were not the most popular in high school. They weren't the prettiest with the best bodies. They were pretty average and maybe slightly above average as far as physical appearance. These girls don't wear the latest clothes and they definitely are not the sexiest even with makeup and tight clothes. The main thing about them is that they have nerdy interests. These women tend to look for men with the same interests.

Now here's the interesting thing. These women check out Mr. Goodbar just like every other woman. A few even hook up with Goodbars. Goodbars though tends to use Awkward Girls for booty calls only. The thing about Awkward Girls is that they are more open to average looking men with modest incomes. They are also open to more authentic men who don't try to use that thing called "game." Awkward Girls tend to be more receptive to a man sincerely trying to get to know them.

Awkward Girls were never part of the in-crowd. They typically never follow the crowd anyway. One thing with women is that their dating and sex choices are influenced by their peers. The Dime picks a man who not only appeals to her but also her friends and greater social circle. The Awkward Girl follows her own counsel. You will see an Awkward Girl with an overweight man, a short man, an introverted man, or a man who looks like he dresses without a mirror. Awkward Girls get with the men they like period. It's been my experience that Awkward Girls do not follow that Select/Non-Select or the more well-known Alpha/Beta paradigms to the same extent as their female peers.

So for the Nerdy Guys, you have a goldmine of women that you are ignoring in your mad chase to get the Dime. The irony is that a few Awkward Girls with the same makeup and high heels can easily compete with the Dimes. They don't because they would rather wear sensible heels and loose pants because they are more comfortable.   Most men get so caught up in acquiring that trophy woman that they miss a diamond right in their mist.   Many Awkward Girls have told me that they actually prefer Nerdy Guys. At the end of the day any man wants a woman who will accept him for the person he is and not some masked personality.

The Pick Up Game is Wack

I got to get something off of my chest. On the Internet there are men and a few women who call themselves teaching that thing called "game." Game as used by these people means primarily using certain techniques to meet and date beautiful women. To be straight up there's a cultural and racial connotation to how the term "game" is used. As used on the Internet by men of a white middle class orientation the meaning is to pick-up women. This includes men of other races who identify with a white male middle class mindset. The term "game" used in Black urban communities means generally knowledge and common sense. Like an older brotha may give a younger brotha advice about what type of job to get. The younger brotha will say that the older brotha gave him "good game." I'm not going to talk about that type of game.

I have real problems with the "game" that is taught on the Internet in blogs, forums, and in expensive seminars held in big hotel rooms. My problem is that the shit don't work for the majority of men who make efforts to learn this "game." I based that comment on not only several statements made by disgruntled men on the Internet who feel like they have been scammed but from dealing with men who have called themselves "Pick Up Artists" (PUAs). I've coached men who have gone through these seminars and classes. Usually I have to deprogram them before I can teach them anything useful. The problem is what the men are being taught is wack to begin with.

From what I have read and been told the main focus of this "game" is to have the confidence to approach beautiful women. Okay I can get with that. Confidence is very important. The issue is that men are being taught to approach as many women as possible. That's wack. Then when these men approach the women they generally have wack ass lines or techniques. I actually saw one video where a man was advised to insult a woman. I'm thinking, "What part of the game is that?" A woman is supposed to get wet because so dorky looking dude walked up to her, asked some indirect questions, and then he insults her? The thought of it sounds stupid. All that really happens is a man usually gets his self-esteem crushed because though rejection can be good, it's only good if it happens occasionally. That way a man can learn from his mistakes and make necessary adjustments. Constant rejection slowly kills a man's spirit.

One thing with constantly approaching women is that it doesn't give a man a chance to really be chosen by a woman. The real process is that a woman chooses a man and then puts herself in a position to be approached by a man. If a woman didn't seduce a man to approach her in most cases he should leave her alone. The **ONLY** time a man should go against this is when the woman may not have seen him and she is just so beautiful and sexy he will regret not approaching. Even then he needs to be direct and polite. He might get rejected but at least he will not kick himself for not trying. Thing is most men are not approaching Dimes. Most approach average to above average women. Quite frankly the women may not be anything special. Regardless, men pay lots of money to have someone tell them to "approach, approach, approach." To be honest approaching several women on any given day can prove to be dangerous.

When I think about men going after women who don't want to be bothered I think of a conversation I had with a young lady I'll call Barbie. The reason I'll call her Barbie is because she was blond haired, blue eyed, with a slim but shapely body. Basically she was at the top of the food chain as far as women go in Western culture. Not only was she beautiful but she was one of the coolest women I've ever met. She was also a professional dog trainer. She would use the word "bitch" in its proper context. She told me a story about a female dog she had. She said a male dog tried to mount her. Only problem was that the female dog wasn't in heat. The female dog killed the male dog. Barbie said, "The bitch killed him." I always remember that because a human female may not, in most cases anyway, try to kill a man coming on to her when she doesn't want to be bothered but she may come close.

There was one time I was at a shopping mall doing a book signing. While I'm sitting there I saw this young dude try to talk to a young Dime. He got aggressive about it and too close to her. She reached into her purse and pulled out a big ass knife. A few minutes later the police came, and the dude was uncooperative. They pepper sprayed him point blank in the face. I know of another incident where a man was being too aggressive with a woman and found out the hard way she was married. Her husband walked up and put a bullet in the dude's head. These PUAs have online videos of them meeting and even kissing women they just met. Many people have called these videos fake. Whether they are or not is up for debate. The issue is that these videos present a false reality. Constantly approaching random women on the street can be hazardous.

I remember talking with a lady friend. We were real cool and joked that we may have been cousins because of where her family is from. One day she had on a tight sweater and tight jeans. I looked at her outfit and asked her how many knives she had on her. In a serious tone she said three. Many women, regardless of race or class background, are armed with a knife or pepper spray. Women have told me they know how to use keys as a weapon. This is especially the case if they are in big cities. Also there has been a lot of

93

noise about specifically criminalizing street harassment. Many men mistakenly attribute the anti-street harassment campaigns to Feminists but really most women do not want to be bothered by men they consider Non-Select.

Let's get past the possible violence and street harassment issues. Most men don't understand how women think. When a woman is approached by a man she didn't choose she wonders why he seems so pressed. A woman knows when a man is trying to get some pussy from her. When most men approach women whether on the street or even in a bar or nightclub they usually look desperate. Many think they are cool, confident, and suave. Women see a man with a "thirsty" look his eyes. In a woman's way of thinking this man must not be getting pussy on the regular. The woman will think that his sex skills are wack. As I've said when women look at a man one of the main things they're asking themselves, "Is he fuckable?" Sex for most women is bad enough. Reportedly the overwhelming majority of men last only three minutes in bed. A woman ain't trying to sign up for that. They look for a man who looks like he knows what he's doing. One reason Goodbar gets attention is that he doesn't look anxious to get pussy. This communicates to the woman that Goodbar must have a satisfying sex life which means his woman is satisfied. That's why many women will have sex with another woman's man. Sometimes if the dick really good the woman will knowingly share her man. This brings me to another point.

Most of these blogs, forums, and videos don't talk about sex. These men will talk about how to meet women and at best get a kiss. Yeah the men want sex but I noticed that these pick-up types really don't talk about sex. Even in reading the reviews for my books and direct feedback nobody really talks about sex. Indeed in *Nice Guys and Players* I devote a whole chapter to sexually satisfying a woman and sexual satisfaction is the main basis of the follow-up book, *Sexual Chemistry.* Yet most reviews and commentary seem to focus more on meeting women. My thing is what is a man going to do once he meets a woman?

The irony of it all is that there is a "game." There are men out there who have developed the art of seduction to a high degree. I'll get into that later when I talk about that drug called Pleasure.

Why Good Guys are Frustrated

One thing I've encountered over the years are frustrated Good Guys. The Good Guys are another subgroup in the Nice Guy category. These men are not nerds. Far from it in fact. These men are also not really Average Joes either. On paper, and according to what women say publically these men should be top of the food chain. Women say they want men with degrees, careers, church going, respectable, and all the good things. The Good Guys have all of that. Yet as a group they may be the most frustrated as far as finding positive relationships. Many of these men will be single and involuntarily celibate for years at a time.

These men know it. It isn't hard to find blogs, forums, videos, and posts on social media with these men complaining about women. Most of the social media comments blame the women. Indeed most the comments straight up attack the women. I get that. Many men have been attracted to a woman who will look them in the eye and say; "You have so many great qualities but I only see you as a friend." They will also say, "You're going to make some woman very lucky one day." Most men just grin and bear it until they see the object of their desire walking around with another man. Not just any man either. The Good Guy has a degree, a career, his own home, and a late model car. The woman who friend zoned him is walking around with an underemployed high school dropout who lives in his mother's basement and doesn't even have a driver's license. A Good Guy can't help but get frustrated and think women as a group have serious issues. It's not the women who have the issues though. It's the Good Guys who have the issue. The issue is entitlement.

Here's a reality. Any random Good Guy can have a woman. The reality is that even though the numbers can be exaggerated, women outnumber men. Now I defined a Good Guy as an educated man with a career and his own home. Even well paid blue collar dudes can be considered Good Guys. There are plenty of women who are sincerely attracted to those type of men. Not so much because of the money but many women are attracted to security. Yeah most women want a good looking man but women are also very pragmatic. They know it's not enough good looking men to go around. Many women are genuinely good with a decent looking man with a job. One young lady told me she wanted a man who had a job and a plan. A decent looking man of modest economic means can get a woman. Indeed many do. Good Guys though are something else.

The thing with Good Guys is that as a result of their education, material goods, and decent incomes they feel they should get the Dimes. Check that, they feel they are entitled to the best looking and sexiest women. I have heard men say this. Collectively they will say, "I have a degree, a career, a home, and a great car, I **DESERVE** a hot woman." The men will want a model with pornstar skills even though physically the men are very average. What amazes me is that most men do not see any problem with this way of thinking. There are several reasons for this.

One of the main reasons is that most men sincerely believe that looks don't matter to women. They feel like they can look anyway they want and women, beautiful women at that, will still have sex with them. I remember one dude who was clinically obese. He had the nerve to say he wouldn't mess with a "fat bitch" to a group of men and women. My thought was that even though he was obese he must have had a big set of balls to make that statement. Thing is he just said out loud what many Good Guys think. The Good Guys think all they need to do is work hard and beautiful women should want them.

Another reason Good Guys get frustrated is organized religion. Regardless of the path most religions emphasize good behavior. The suggestion is that when a man behaves a certain way he is rewarded not only in an afterlife place but while he is living. Many men feel like since they at least try to do the right thing according to their paths they should not only be blessed materially but they should get the best women. Most paths have something to say about getting a good woman. A good woman in a man's mind means good-looking and submissive. Most religions emphasize men being the leader and women following. The Good Guy who is a faithful and contributing member of his church, mosque, or temple expects the women he deals with to follow along with their God's plan. The thing is many women do follow along with the plan. Just not the pretty face woman with the phat booty and serious dick sucking skills. Yes I said dick sucking skills.

Many of these Good Guys are frustrated because they want a woman who is a lady in public and a hoe in the bedroom. Many Good Guys may get a decent woman who is very much in line with being proper in public. Often time they are duds in the bedroom. No matter how religious or moral a Good Guy is, the primal man in him wants that woman who gets his dick rock hard. For example many Good Guys talk trash about low class women. If you listen to them talk or read what they say on blogs, forums, and social media its obvious most of the attention is focused on ratchet women. It's some bullshit though. Most of these Good Guys, regardless of race and nationality, are middle class. Some are even upper middle class flirting with being affluent. Why would these Good Guys be worried about what project dwelling, trailer park living, women are doing?

Stop and think about it for a second.

The only reason Good Guys would worry about low class women is that many are not only physically attractive but sexually attractive as well. A man will only be concerned about something that he wants. Low class women, however, tend to be attracted to low class men. The only exception is when a low class woman is also a gold digger. Good Guys ain't thinking like that though. Good Guys think they are on top of the pyramid and that they should get all of the pretty and sexy women regardless of social class limitations. That's that entitlement piece.

One thing with Good Guys is that their expectations don't match reality. They expect women to act a certain way. When women don't act the way the men want then it's felt that the women have issues. In listening to these men and reading their blogs and forum posts it becomes obvious that Good Guys are trying to force women to behave a certain way. Something I've known since I was a little boy was that a man cannot make a woman do anything without use of force. I've dealt with women by controlling my reaction to what they do. As long as a person's actions doesn't interfere with my life I let them do them. Many Good Guys try to different methods to change a woman's behavior. Basically they want the women to let them out of the friendzone. Shit ain't gonna happen. Until a Good Guy deals with these entitlement issues he will continue to live a life of frustration.

The Drug Called Pleasure

It's interesting to listen to Non-Select men complain about the choices women make. They can't for the life of them see the appeal of a Player or Bad Boy. They think the women are the ones with issues and they should go for the Good Guys. Even the women feel this way. Many women will wonder why they can't seem to fall in love with a gainfully employed, church going, and respectful man. Instead the women are going crazy over a man who barely texts them, who may put them down, and will have multiple other women. Even when women kick a Player to the curb they usually end up swooning for another Player. What's the issue? From "A Player's Eyes" the answer is simple. A woman will put up with a Player, Bad Boy, or Dog for one reason and one reason alone: That drug called **PLEASURE**.

Using the term, "Mr. Goodbar" is not a random piece of slang. One woman said it meant a man had a good dick. Not really. "Mr. Goodbar" is more of an allegory of what women experience with this type of man. Most women like chocolate and I don't mean in a racial sense. Give most women something with chocolate in it, be it a candy bar or an ice cream sundae and they will derive great **PLEASURE** from eating that chocolate. Some women will even get mild orgasms from eating chocolate. Mr. Goodbar is a human version of that piece of chocolate. She wants to indulge as much as possible in his presence. Her body chemistry will literally change when she is around this man. This chemistry produces a state of euphoria in the woman that is similar to the feeling a person gets when they drink alcohol. The woman in Mr. Goodbar's presence is in a state of romantic intoxication. An overwhelming majority of women are addicted to getting this feeling of intoxication, this euphoria, this **PLEASURE**. Women are just like junkies in this regard. Instead of tapping their arms for their fix, they tap their thighs. The Players and Bad Boys are not delivering this drug on a street corner. These men are delivering this drug in bedrooms, offices, storage rooms, and sometimes in back alleys.

Here's something deep for you. The key to where a man stands with women is his ability to deliver this drug, this euphoria, this intoxication. We will call this drug, **"Pleasure."** The biggest mistake most men make is not knowing how women see them. Many men see themselves as Alpha Males. They will have kick-ass manager jobs or successful businesses making big money. They will be above average in looks and height. They will have homes and cars. Same type of men I described in the previous section. Yet they will struggle in their relationships with women. They may get sex but not from the Dimes. They may have to settle with the Plain Jane with a slight attitude. These men don't get the best women because they are unable to deliver the Pleasure. When the average woman is looking at a man she is looking for clues that he can deliver that good stuff. Many men despite what they have going on for them materially and how confident they are they don't think in terms of delivering Pleasure. Indeed most men when they get a little bit of money feel like women should fall over them. They see the woman as an accessory to their lives, a trophy to be won if the woman is a Dime. Knowing that women judge men according to their ability to deliver Pleasure it then shines a different light on the sexual hierarchy of how women see men.

Mr. Goodbar is the top of the sexual pyramid. Goodbars typically have above average body builds and facial features. Most Goodbars wouldn't make money as male models but women will describe them as extremely sexy. A Goodbar's primary skill is the ability to deliver the Pleasure. He's knows how to push a woman's romantic buttons. One of the main ways he does this is by not chasing women. Most often women will chase Goodbar. Women see that Goodbar can deliver the Pleasure. Goodbar though doesn't give the

Pleasure for free. Goodbar will make a woman work for that Pleasure. The method is simple. The Goodbar will give a woman just a little Pleasure. He might see a Dime in passing as he is out and about every day. While every other man is breaking their necks to talk to the woman, Goodbar ignores her. This isn't a game tactic. Goodbars tend to be men who have been around a lot of beautiful women so the Dime may not stand out to him. The Dime notices that this one man is ignoring her. He may not even be that good-looking to her at first but it intrigues her that he ignores her, so she will work harder to get his attention. Goodbar starts to notice her after she wears a short tight dress for the fifth day in a row. He says hi and keeps it moving. The Dime gets Pleasure from being acknowledged by him. After he only says hi to her a couple of more times, she approaches him and starts a conversation. He's fun to talk to so she gets more Pleasure. She finds him sexy so she gets Pleasure every time she sees him. He even starts to look better to her. She starts imagining different scenarios where the two of them have sex. They talk more and she hints about dating. Goodbar, who picked up on her interest a while ago, asks her out on a date. They end the date at his apartment. The Dime has several orgasms. He tells her he has other women but she doesn't care. The Dime is hooked on the Pleasure.

Next on the sexual pyramid are the Masked Men. Most people think that the Masked Men are at the top of the pyramid. That's because Mr. Goodbar operates in the shadows. Mr. Goodbar fucks many women who have boyfriends or husbands. Most prefer to keep a low profile. Plus as I said Goodbars may be handsome with nice bodies but they are not going to have their pictures passed around on social media. The Masked Man will have their pictures passed around. The Masked Man can deliver a watered down version of Pleasure. He has to mix his product with some money and status. A man puts on the mask when he becomes on the surface what women say they want. Women publically say they want a man who's handsome, tall, educated with a lot of money. Few men can become that mask. These men can't deliver the same level of pleasure. I remember a lady friend told me about a man she met. She said, "Rom he looks right, says the right things, and he has money. Something's missing though." The thing missing was that this man couldn't give her the same level of Pleasure that a Bad Boy was giving her.

An interesting aspect with the Masked Men is that good looks can be a mask. A really good-looking Masked Man may think he is Mr. Goodbar. Looks will always arouse any woman to some extent. What happens though is that a woman will meet a good-looking Masked Man but be turned off sexually once he opens his mouth. In other words he isn't bringing the Pleasure beyond the looks. Looks though important only take a man so far. In this case a woman may still deal with a Masked Man because of his money and status. She may even marry him. In time though once she gets past the looks, money, and status the woman may not like the man underneath the mask. This is why women may cheat or leave an otherwise good-looking man with money.

Mr. Goodbar and the Masked Men are considered Select because of their ability to deliver the Pleasure. That is the most important consideration for a man to be placed in the Select category. Social factors such a money and status only play minor parts. The next two categories are Non-Select because of their inability to deliver the Pleasure.

Next on the sexual pyramid are the Nice Guys. These are the Good Guys, the Lames, the Nerds, and the Average Joes. These are the men who inhabit the dreaded friend zone. Women, especially Dimes, welcome platonic relationships with these men. These men are good for a hangout buddy, a shoulder to cry on, and a dependable person to help move furniture. The problem is that these men don't know that the traits that make a man a good human being are not the same traits that will make a woman's vagina tingle. These men do not deliver the Pleasure. Most don't have a concept of the Pleasure. The reason is that for most of their lives Nice Guys were told many lies about the sexual nature of women. They were told that as long as they were gentlemen a good woman, (i.e. Dime) would appreciate their generous personalities and reward them with sex. After a while these men may become bitter as they watch the object of their desire swoon in the arms of a Bad Boy. When Nice Guys do get the girl it is usually after she has had been dogged enough by Goodbars and Masked Men. Nice Guys usually end up with damaged women whose beauty and shape has faded along with two kids fathered by deadbeat pretty boys. Many Nice Guys eventually rebel against this state of affairs in various ways such as travelling to other countries to find a mate or by withdrawing from the dating scene all together.

Last on the pyramid are the Gamesmen. Gamesmen are interesting because as a group they tend to think they are on top of the sexual pyramid. These are the men who use what they consider "game" to get women. First of all Gamesmen don't deliver Pleasure. The Gamesman really has one thing going for him, persistence. The Gamesman will play the numbers game and hit on as many women as possible. To be clear they do get sex. Two types of women generally fall for the "game." The first is a woman who is socially inept who may not have the looks to attract a Goodbar, Masked Man, or a Nice Guy. Gamesmen, who are also known as Thirsty Men, are not very picky. They take what they can get. They may act like they are getting Dimes in online forums and while they are lying on their dicks with their boys but in real life they are messing with a homely girl who lacks common sense. The second type of woman a Gamesman gets will be an Easy Girl. There are plenty of Easy Girls walking around. Even a few Easy Dimes. A Gamesman will get with one of these women and will think his "game" got him over. Naw, the reality is that an Easy Girl will pretty much fuck any man who shows an interest. Easy Girls let men choose them. Even Nice Guys hook up with Easy Girls thinking they got a prize until a paternity test shows that they are not the father.   Most women reject the Gamesman.

Now I know many men won't agree with what I just wrote. They'll only disagree because they are not looking at this with "A Player's Eyes."   I don't talk out the side of my neck. I've had personal conversations with literally thousands of women. Now I say this a lot and many men would think this is impossible.   Keep in mind that I've had jobs which required me to talk to plenty of women. Also I have over twenty years of vending and sales experience where I'm constantly interacting with women because of my books. I've also dated several hundred women.   In addition I'm getting insight from other true Players.   Let's look at the Player angle a bit more.

I've had the opportunity to interact with true Players since I was little.   These are men who I witnessed getting women. I've known quite a few of the women that got with these men. It would be the women telling me they had sex with these men. I've had women actually introduce me to the Players.   In talking with these men which at this point has been several dozen I found one thing in common with all of them: they loved to deliver the Pleasure.   These men **ALWAYS** spoke in terms of satisfying the women.   They always spoke in terms of being affectionate with women.   I knew one blatant womanizer who said he liked to hold women after sex. I also witnessed two women physically fight over him.

Most men do not think in terms of satisfying women. Most men talk in terms of what women can do for them. It's no wonder that 75 percent of men will ejaculate in three minutes. How is that satisfying a woman? That woman, no matter how much she loves and cares for the man, will look for a secret lover who can last long enough to give her an orgasm. Ask me how I know. There's been so many situations where I was at a woman's place and her man calls and she's like, "Rom you gotta be quiet it's Elmo." To this day I refer to a woman's boyfriend as Elmo. Yeah I used to roll dirty but I digress.

A problem I see is that when men do talk in terms publically of satisfying a woman they are called Simps. It seems like they are kissing up to a woman by putting her on a pedestal. Most of these men who call other men Simps don't get sex on the regular and are hiding behind a macho façade. These types of men are the biggest Simps because they will empty their bank account for a gold digging Dime. It happens a lot.

Here's the deal. If a man satisfies a woman and give her that good Pleasure she will return the favor a hundred fold. It's like putting $1000 into an investment account and a few months later that $1000 has become $10,000. The beauty of that drug called Pleasure is that once women get it they **WANT** to give it right back. Many men out here complain that women aren't submissive. Give women just a sample of Pleasure and she will not only be submissive but she will wake you up in the morning with not only a big breakfast wearing nothing but a thong but also a blow job. Many women get Pleasure by giving Pleasure. But men are stupid out here. They don't think in terms of giving women that Pleasure.

Many men think that thing called game is the great equalizer to not having great looks. Game ain't shit compared to the Pleasure. Often people see a Dime with a man who is ugly, short, or overweight. They assume he has money or game. They get closer to the situation and find out he has neither. What that man does have is the ability to give Pleasure. I knew a woman who was dealing with a Nice Guy. She wasn't pressed about him. He chasing her was more an ego boost than anything else. She finally consented to sex with him and her mind was blown. She said, "Elmo got skills." Elmo got upgraded from Nice Guy to Mr. Goodbar.

If I gathered to every single Goodbar I know and put them on a stage in front of several men and women and asked people to pick out the players most of the Goodbars wouldn't be picked. Only a few who were actual models may be picked. Much of the conventional wisdom about men who are lovers of many women is wrong. That's why dating coaches who try to teach skills to clueless men can't really show any success. The dating coaches are teaching the wrong things. A man who isn't conventionally good-looking or popular can't win by simply approaching numerous women. A true seduction takes time. A true Player meets a woman on his job or in his social circle and slowly gives her doses of Pleasure. After a while the woman gets turned on by simply

110

seeing the man because he always says or does something that makes her feel good. Once he sees that she is hooked he can ask for the pussy at his leisure.

Now I know some men are reading this thinking, "Rom tell us how to give the Pleasure." I already did in my books. So many men read my stuff looking for techniques that they had some familiarity with that they missed what I actually wrote. Some didn't think I knew what I was talking about. That's okay. Several men I know who got what I wrote have more women than they know what to do with. The Pleasure is the secret. Men will have trouble with women until learning to deliver the Pleasure becomes as important as making money and watching ballgames.

Lovers of Many Women

One thing I find interesting is when men lie on their dicks about the number of women they've been with. A rule of thumb I have is that if a man says he's been with 50 women the real number may be 25. Of course very few men have been with 25 women. Here's a reality, the average man will only have sex with five women in his life. There's some men who have had sex with hundred or so women. If you dig deeper you will find the majority of these women were prostitutes and escorts. Very few men have had sex with over ten women that they didn't have to pay for. That includes gold digging situations because that is really just another form of prostitution.

People don't realize how deep it for a man to sleep with a great number of women in his lifetime. That's why a lot of men go crazy if they get dumped by their girlfriends or divorced from their wives. Once a man finds that one woman who will fuck him on the regular he wants to hold on tight. Many men will lock down their women for that reason. Even when a man cheats he just has one other mistress. The average man will have about thirty women in his life who will feel a natural attraction to him. Thing is he's not going to have sex with all thirty if he even meets them. Most people will not meet all the persons most naturally attracted to them. The man may be lucky to meet his thirty but fifteen of them will be in relationships. He will not be naturally attracted to ten of them. The timing will be off with at least two of the women. So he may hook up with three women.

I'm not saying anything new to men. Despite how much trash men talk they know a whole bunch of women ain't feeling them like that. That's why a lot of men will go back to women from their past they had a relationship with. One situation I'm familiar with is when this man had a woman feeling him when he was young. He didn't treat her right even though she was the only woman giving him some play. Eventually she moved on and married a man who treated her the way she deserved. Dude found out the hard way that other women weren't as tolerant of his trifling ass. So the bamma tried to get back with the woman. Many men are in the same boat. That's why most men try to lock that pussy down. Indeed a lot of game passed around in urban communities is about control. A man who has multiple women doesn't really feel the need to lock one down. If she

113

wants to bounce he lets her go. He might not notice she left. Yeah it can be like that.

I want to talk about the men who legitimately get multiple women. I've known a few dozen verifiable Lovers of Many Women (LMW). I say verifiable because as I stated many men lie on their dicks. I verified these men not through anything they said. I was able to find out they were legitimate by knowing their women, watching how women responded to them, and in a few cases knowing how many baby mamas they had. If a man has multiple babies by several women he is a legitimate LMW. One thing about these men is that they go against virtually every piece of dating and seduction advice on the Internet or taught in seminars. They are even outside of what I teach in my books.

On the surface it may seem Goodbars and LMWs are interchangeable. Many Goodbars are LMWS but not all. Many Goodbars will be kept men for women with resources. Some Goodbars for whatever reason may only deal with a few women. A high sex count does not automatically make a man a Goodbar. A Masked Man can be a LMW. If he know how to use his money and status to play a woman right he can get away with not paying for the pussy. A few Gamesmen can be LMWs. I never said game doesn't exist. It's just not being taught in the public sphere. A person can only be mentored in the real game. The mentor is usually a father or an older relative. A really good Gamesman can get a high sex count even though he's Non-Select.

Even a Nice Guy can be a LMW. It would depend heavily on what which subgroup he's in. For example a sensible Good Guy can get a lot of sex if he deals with women who are a bit lower on the economic scale than he is. A man who has his own home, car, and steady job in an economically depressed area looks very good to women who are struggling on minimum wage. Now if he has a decent body build he is like gold to the women around him. Of course most of the women won't be Dimes but to a LMW it doesn't matter. Let's talk about some realities.

It cracks me up when dating coaches sell the dream that any man with the right techniques can live a life where he is having sex with dozens of Dimes. It's a straight up scam. First of all the only men who will get to have sex with multiple Dimes will be musicians and pro athletes. This is because they are having sex with groupies. That's a subculture right there. To be a groupie a woman has to be drop dead gorgeous because she is competing with other beautiful women. The musicians and pro athletes are having sex with these women because the women are coming to them. These men aren't approaching these women on the street. These women are right there at the hotels or backstage at the arenas. That's a whole different world. Some dork who didn't kiss a girl as a teenager isn't going to get it like that no matter how much money he spends.

I'm just being raw.

Any man who has slept with more than 20 women in his life has slept with a few women who he might not want to be seen in public with. The average LMW may have slept with one Dime out of 50 women. I'm talking about a woman who has a pretty face, killer body, and sex appeal. Those women are **RARE.** I've written several times I have dealt with thousands of women in my life. Outside of my cousins I have dealt with only 40 - 50 true Dimes. The number only goes to a hundred when dealing with women one level below the Dimes. Most women out here are average to slightly above average. The best most men have potential for is a woman with a decent face and body.

One thing that every LMW will do is find the beauty in the women he deals with. To me men chasing Dimes are being unrealistic and setting themselves up for a life of disappointment. I was talking with a young Goodbar one time. We talking about how many men sleep on the women out here because they don't look like models or pornstars. He said many of these average looking women had some good pussy and cooperative personalities. I agreed with him. There are a lot of untapped (pun intended) women out here. The LMW will see the potential. I'm going to share a secret about myself.

Earlier I wrote that beauty doesn't faze me. I notice it like any other man but it does nothing for me. I pay more attention to a woman's sex appeal. Some of the sexiest women I have known in my life would be considered average or even ugly to most men. But to a LMW or to any sexually attuned man these women were top tier. When I say sexually attuned that means the man isn't just using his eyes with the woman. He's feeling the woman. Most men don't feel a woman because they are not connected to their dicks. If you ask most men if they can feel their dicks without using their hands they would say no. These men are typically sexually repressed and more in their heads. A sexually attuned man is aware of his genitals and will respond naturally to the sexual presence of a sensual woman and not just to her image. I remember I was doing a book signing one time. It was in a mall and my table was set up just outside of the store. I was talking with a man and a woman. While we were talking a tall woman walked past us. Her face was nothing special and she wore just a loose t-shirt and jeans. When she walked by her butt was big and round and swaying very seductively. The man and I were speechless. The woman at the table had to say, "Damn!" for us. The woman dripped sex appeal even though she was dressed plain.

The LMW gets many women because he hones in a woman's sex appeal regardless of what the outer package looks like. This is important because in order for a man to have sex with multiple women those multiple women have to want to have sex with him. The LMW is able to arouse women sexually. The key is finding it in any woman. Many men will chase that pretty girl. Then if they are lucky enough to catch or rather she allows herself to be caught they find out the hard way that she is a dud in the bedroom. You know what, even though I generally say I don't teach game I'm going to give the men some real street game.

In terms of sex, a Dime doesn't have to be good in bed. Men are going to chase her regardless. Men want to be seen with her. She is a trophy. Men get more out of the attainment than actually being with her. I've had men complain to me about bad sex with a Dime on more than one occasion. Most men will have sex with her even if she just lays there all the time. Plus when a woman is physically attractive she doesn't have to develop any special sexual skills. For what? The Dime usually has a roster of men ready to get at her.

Now contrast that with the Plain Jane or even ugly girl. They have to bring something extra. I wish I had a dime every time some dude told me that a plain face, fat girl rocked his world in the bedroom. Men with real experience with multiple women will go for the less physically attractive woman because they know she will be more adventurous sexually. That's why when many men cheat it's not with a drop dead gorgeous woman. The mistress rarely looks better than the wife. That's because the wife is for public viewing while the mistress is strictly for sex.

That why many very handsome men end up with plain women. People always look and think, "why her?" It probably wasn't her personality. She pussy whipped that bamma. Funny thing about that dynamic is that it works the other way too.

People will constantly see a beautiful woman with a man they consider ugly. The first thing people think is that he has money or game. Neither one. I've talked with many

118

of these women. They'll say, "He isn't much to look at but he can fuck." This brings me to another point about LMWs.

I have written earlier that Goodbars were not necessarily extremely handsome. Same thing applies to LMWs. All the rules are thrown out the window with these guys. There are two general schools of thought as far as what it takes to get women in the dating advice industry. The first is that a man needs to have looks, money, and status (LMS) to get women. Not one LMW I have encountered would stand out as far as looks. They wouldn't be mistaken for pretty boys and even the women who slept with them would call them average. Body wise these men tended to be built solid but not necessarily muscular. A few had noticeable guts. These men had modest incomes as a group and lacked status. According to the LMS School these men shouldn't be getting any attention.

The second school of thought is that men need game to get women. LMWs lack what is popularly considered game. Indeed I've talked with a few LMWs about "game" and they looked at me like I was making stuff up. LMWs just click with women. They don't do anything special. They meet women very easily and can have good conversations without the need to use any special techniques.

The LMW has sexual charisma. He gives off a vibe that he would be good in bed. He doesn't look like he will judge a woman for not being a Dime. The LMW will find the sexy in the pudgy but shapely Plain Jane. He'll bring the freak out in a conservative church girl. Most importantly a

LMW is never without companionship as women will approach him.

I bring up the LMW because the reality is that there are men who have figured out how sleep with multiple women. These are unique men. They have a gift that men would pay millions to acquire. Think about how much men spend on prostitution, sex tourism, mail order brides, or being a sugar daddy. We're talking in the billions. Yet you have men who get decent women and also occasionally Dimes without spending a cent. That's some powerful shit right there.

Incompatibility and Unrealistic Expectations

One of the first relationship books I read back in the day was by a gentleman named Don Spears. The book was called, **"In Search of Goodpussy."** Yeah that was the title. The gist of the book was about how men, particularly Black men, were looking for love in their relationships. Don Spears covered a lot of issues that are still relevant today even though his book was published in 1991. One chapter was entitled, "Incompatibility and Unrealistic Expectations." In that chapter he said the biggest reasons relationships fail is that the two people were incompatible with each other and that they had unrealistic expectations that such a relationship would work. Let's look at the unrealistic expectation piece first.

The biggest single problem in male/female relationships is that most people are not realistic in searching for a mate. You have plain looking, average shaped women with boring personalities thinking they can get a top tier male. These women will not only reject men who are more in their league as far as looks and personality but they will do so with an attitude. Even when they manage to hook up with a Select Man in most cases they are not really compatible. Bomb sex doesn't mean that two people need to be together outside the bedroom. Dude could just have that good dick which he shares with five other women. Yet Plain Jane thinks its love when she is really just a cool booty call. Then when Plain Jane realizes that Mr. Goodbar doesn't love her all men become dogs until she starts to swoon in the arms of another sexy dude.

The bad part in all of this is that her Plain Jane girlfriends will encourage her in this. They know their girl don't look good in those yoga pants and that she should stop doing her own hair. They will be the main ones saying that pretty boy don't know what he's missing out on. Her girlfriends ain't being honest with her because they want to believe they can get a rich pretty boy too.

The irony is that Plain Jane will have an Average Joe who is feeling her basic looking self, even with the muffin top. She can even be in a relationship with him. Average Joe treats her well, holds her hand in public, and is even decent in bed. Of course her jealous girlfriends start getting in her ear about how she could do better. Average Joe is just a regular looking dude who could stand to lose some weight and needs to buy clothes from places other than a discount store. Plus her girlfriends are jealous that Jane has a man at all as no one is blowing up their phones or liking their pictures on social media. Jane starts listening to her girlfriends and kicks Average Joe to the curb for some minor shit. Story don't end there though.

Few women will kick a man to the curb without having another man in mind. Jane has been checking out this tall muscular dude she has been seeing around the mall where she works, Dexter Goodbar. Dude starts being friendly to Jane after she had said hi to him every time she saw him for a month. Her sexual interest shows all over her face so Dexter marks her for sex somewhere down the road. Jane, being in her fantasy world thinks she has a chance so after getting rid of Average Joe she fixes her hair a bit and starts wearing body shaping garments under her clothes. She even shops for new outfits and finally joins a gym. Dexter takes notice and gives her his number. She blows up his phone and friends him on social media. They eventually have sex after he invites her over to chill. They go hot and heavy for a month before he decides to kick her to the curb. A Dime made herself available to him and he didn't want to be seen in public with Jane anyway.

Plain Jane goes into depression because she realized that she was just a sex toy for Goodbar as he never went out with her. To add to that depression she finds out that Average Joe is now going out with one of the women who told her to get rid of Average Joe to begin with.   The problem was Plain Jane wasn't realistic as to who she was and the type of man she could actually get.

It's just as bad for men.   There are many Non-Select men who can probably get a decent woman.   That woman will not be a Dime though.   For every woman who is insistent on getting an A-1 man there is a woman who has enough common sense to be good with an Average Joe. Thing is, many Average Joes don't want those women. Dude is plain-looking or even ugly.   He isn't tall, doesn't have an athletic body, and has very little style as far as dressing.   His personality is dull.   Yet many of these men because they have a steady job with decent pay think they should get a Dime.   Not just a Dime but a Dime who will fuck them like a pornstar.   I've heard numerous Average Joes articulate this in one form or another.

These men don't seem to grasp that a beautiful woman who is good at sex will want a similar man.   A woman know she got a pretty face, firm breasts, a small waist, and a phat round ass.   Good genes gave her the face and three hours in the gym, six days a week gave her the body. Her hard work on her job supplemented by men with big credit limits paid for her hair and tight dresses. The fuck will this Dime want with some homely, pudgy, or skinny dude who can't engage her in a stimulating conversation?   There are some men who honestly think a Dime wants a fucked up looking dude humping her for three minutes.   A Dime more so than a Plain Jane wants Mr. Goodbar.   The more a

124

woman is in good physical shape especially internally the more she will be aroused by a man with a great body.

Many Average Joes, Good Guys, Nerdy Guys, and Gamesmen think they have a real chance with a Dime. It's easier to lie to themselves instead of doing the work necessary to become desirable. After the Non-Select men get rejected for the umpteenth time they either withdraw from the game or take to the Internet where they can call women bitches and thots.

The problem comes down to people not staying in their lane. Many men and women want that ideal figure as opposed to the person they can actually get. So many men and women are chasing unicorns and then get depressed when they don't find that special person. It's not that the person don't exist, it's just that the person may not look like someone's romantic ideal on the surface. I'm not saying go for someone who is physically unattractive to you. It's just that often when people are chasing Dexter Goodbar or Julie Dime they pass over decent people right in their midst. People who are not only decent looking but have compatible personalities.

So many people out here are looking for surface shit. Thing is being attracted to the outer shell is normal and necessary in a balanced relationship. Notice I said balanced. Fuck political correctness, a person needs to like to look at their mates. The problem is that people put so much stock in the outer that they miss the inner. That's why a lot of men and women get burned. You might like a person's face

125

and body but what if that person practices a value system that is in opposition to your own? The physical aspect of the relationship will be good for a few months but problems will occur once the value systems and personalities start to show themselves.

I've known several Dimes in my life. Some were compatible to my personality and some were not. It didn't make anyone bad but any relationship with the incompatible women beyond sex would have caused me mental anguish. So many men chase these incompatible women anyway. Yeah they look good to family and friends but behind closed doors many men are getting their asses kicked emotionally. I've had men tell me the vile shit some women did to them and they would always end the conversation with, "she had a phat ass though."

I've known a few extremely handsome men in my life. It would seem like they had it made. Nope they got their foul shit too. I've not only known these men, I've known their women as well. The women found out the hard way that all that glitters is not gold. Piercing eyes and a pretty smile have fucked up many a woman's head. The problem was that women didn't think in terms of compatibility. A handsome man making a woman laugh is just that, a handsome man making a woman laugh. If a man look good enough he could say "poo poo" in a monotone voice and the woman will think it's the funniest and sexiest thing she has ever heard. A muscular body can make a man a comic genius to a horny woman. This doesn't speak to whether they are

126

compatible yet a woman will think they are right for each other.

Ultimately people need to balance how they choose a mate. First they have to be realistic. If a man is 5'7", twenty pounds overweight, with an average face, and sporadic employment history it would be unrealistic for him to think that a 5'11" Dime with a killer body and high paying job is going to want him. The woman who might feel him may be plain looking with extra weight around her stomach. Thing is she is shorter than him and will tolerate his inability to keep a steady job as long as he treats her right. She even thinks he's cute.

If a woman is plain faced, slim, without any curves or breasts, and dull personality it isn't realistic to think she'll get a tall muscular man with money and charisma. Only in poorly written romance novels does this happen. If she does get such a man he will likely use her to do things sexually his girlfriend or wife doesn't want to do. The best man for this woman is someone who likes slim and quiet women who may be average looking with a modest income and equally dull personality.

Bottom line is that people have to have realistic expectations of potential mates and they have to be compatible.

A Player's Eyes

There's so much I could write about but in the age of 140 word statements and 15 second videos I would start losing the reader's attention.   I can always do more books. People are going to get different things from what I wrote. Some people will have their mind blown.   Some will be relieved that someone else has articulated their own experiences.   Some people going to think I'm making up shit to look good.   I want to address that last point.

The reality is that only a small percentage of men have experienced what I have with dealing with women.   The majority struggle in their relationships.   That's even when they can get one.   Many men don't believe anything they haven't personally experienced. I've told men that I've always been approached by Dimes and they think I'm lying. The reason is they and their associates have never been approached by a beautiful woman. I mentioned to a couple of men that several women have showed up to my living space in the past without wearing underwear. No way have they said, because it hasn't happened to them. I tell them I have to think hard about how many women I've had some sexual contact with in my life. They automatically think I'm bullshitting because they remember the three women they have been with.

My point is that my experience is not like the majority of men. I thought it was at first until I realized that my peer groups have included LMWs and Goodbars since the age of 7. I thought it was normal as an 8 year old to have little girls take their panties down and show boys their vaginas. My mother had to explain sex to me after I told her I witnessed a little girl sucking a little boy's dick. I knew the concept of slowly making love to a girl as a ten year old. I hadn't reached puberty yet but I had developed the discipline to not get excited by grown women walking around me with nothing on but their panties. Yeah, I had an interesting childhood. I've seen a lot. I was forced to think like an adult as a child. To this day it takes a great effort on my part to tolerate people in adult bodies who behave like children. As far as my environment, intervention by child protective services was necessary. That's all I'll say about that.

The thing I wanted to do with this book was give men and women a different perspective on sexual relationships. When most men speak on relationship dynamics they come from a place of disappointment and bitterness. Most men are trying to figure out why they don't have the relationships they want. It could be men who are involuntary celibate. It could be men who are fighting for the right to see their children after a divorce. There are men who study game and self-improvement in order to be more attractive to women. Many men simply withdraw from interacting with women. There's still more angles.

Many men try a different approach. They worship women as goddesses. There are subcultures of men that actually do this. Thing is they still don't get the love or attention they desire from women. Some try to be White Knights and still have trouble. I don't live in those worlds. The irony is that I thought I did live in those worlds. In retrospect I realize that my tendency was to compare myself to more seasoned players. I didn't know how good I had it.

Now I know many men have read through this book wanting to find my secrets. They don't doubt what I wrote. They want to know how to be me. One issue out here is that men have made it dealing with women more complicated than it has to be. So let me share my secrets.

I was able to have various levels of relationships with women for two basic reasons. The first reason is that most of the women I dealt with found me to be physically attractive. I looked good to them. That's it. No game or anything.   Before some dumbass calls me conceited I said I looked good to the women I dealt with.   Most women who didn't find me good looking didn't mess with me.   A man doesn't need to be drop dead gorgeous to get women.   There are women who are going to be naturally attracted to him regardless of what he looks like.   He could have stringy hair, acne, a lopsided head with one tooth in his mouth, and there will be at least one woman who thinks he's the most beautiful man she's ever seen.   All I did was pay attention to how women would look at me and listen to how they complimented my physical features.   If they commented that my eyes looked nice or that I had a nice body I start thinking about how they would look with their phat asses waving in the air.   It take more than looks though and to a few women I only looked "aight."

The second reason I was able to get women was that I have a cool personality.   Even women who weren't physically attracted to me said I was cool to be around. Women found me to be very likeable.   The beauty of it was that I didn't have to pretend.   One thing about me is that I have a very high tolerance for people's quirkiness as long as they aren't childish about it.   They could be as eccentric as they want to be as long they were relatively mature.   What many men don't know about Dimes is that many are undercover Awkward Girls.   I allow women to be themselves around me.   I don't judge them even in cases where childishness creeps in.   For many women this enhanced my physical attractiveness.

131

So two things. No "game." No sneaky techniques. I was just real. If I couldn't pull a woman being who I was as a man then I wasn't meant to be with her. One thing I always looked for with women was simply compatibility. That thing an old school Mack I knew called an instant click. I never forced shit with a woman. We either clicked or we didn't. Yeah there were some I initially wished we had clicked but later down the road I realized I dodged many a bullet.

So yes I have a different perspective on relationships. Even dealing with Dimes. Most men want the Dimes and they will listen to other clueless men about how to get a Dime. Here's something interesting about me. I've been approached by many women in my life. The overwhelming majority of these women were Dimes or women who men would rate as Eights. While most men are figuring out how to approach these drop dead gorgeous women, the same women would routinely initiate conversations with me. One thing about Dimes is that they tend to be aggressive when they are interested in a man. So I've known plenty in life in addition to my family members. When I say I've known them, I've known them. They would tell me everything. One thing they would tell about was how "game" didn't work with them.

Understand this with Dimes. They have seen everything. A 25 year-old Dime has been hit on by every type of man from a lecherous relative to a rich businessman. Dudes who think they can get over on Dimes are deluded.

The game does not work. At least not with Dimes. Even when it seems like a man has got a woman using "game" it really a case of she thinking he was cute anyway. The best thing with a Dime is to be straight up. If you have to approach, just walk up, tell her you find her attractive, and would like to get to know her. Go to a coffee shop right then if you both have time. Dimes catch so much bullshit that straight honesty is the best "game." It's worked well for me the few times I've approached beautiful women in the streets.

"A Player's Eye's" though isn't about how to get women. It's not about talking about the "game." It's even more than about sexual dynamics in relationships. It about seeing something from another perspective. Like I said I really haven't experienced the same disappointments with women that other men have. Yes I've been dumped and had some negative experiences but the positive experiences were more plentiful. It would be easy for me to simply ignore the plight of less fortunate men. To be honest I would rather be writing the science fiction novel I've been wanting to write for a few years. Thing is I've read many accounts by Non-Select men. I've talked with plenty. It's been helpful to me to see and respect their perspective. A good friend said to me one time, "Rom you get your share of women and everybody else's too." When he said that it made me think about how many women I may have been stringing along thinking they would get more from me. There were men out there who wanted to love these women. Those same women who would

133

hold out hope that my off the chains, complicated ass would act right. It's some deep shit.

One time I sat down and thought what if I hadn't had sex with a few of the women I've been with? What if that beautiful Dime with the big legs never had her legs wrapped around my back? What if I never felt what it was like to give a woman such a strong orgasm that she trembled for twenty minutes? What if I never had those experiences? Then I thought some men will never experience those things. One of the most beautiful things a man can experience is a woman who fully surrenders to him sexually. The look in her eyes that says, "Be strong. Be my warrior, my hunter, my leader, my healer." Just to admire the female body is a great feeling. Perhaps no feeling can match the first time a man physically penetrates a woman especially if they had developed an emotional bond. That gasp when first entering a woman is incredible. A feeling enhanced when the seduction was slow and steady over a period of time. Damn! Now that's goodpussy!

Many men won't know that feeling. Even if they find a woman often the sex is mediocre because they really don't want each other. They both may fantasize about other people in order to reach some level of satisfaction.

I want people to finish reading this book with a sense of seeing things another way. To know that there is more possibilities. It's nothing special about me. Any looks I have is the result of hard work. I stay physically active and I'm disciplined about how and what I eat. Over the years through trial and error I figured out which clothing styles enhanced my sex appeal the best.   I have worked and will continue to work to develop my character.   I'm a work in progress.

I hope the reader got something from my perspective. I've given a glimpse of what it's like to see from my eyes. The picture is not always pretty but it's real.   Maybe through my eyes you can see your reflection and make the changes you need to make to find your own happiness.

Peace and Blessings,

Rom Wills

About the Author

      Who is Rom Wills? I have had many words used to describe me. I've been called mysterious, brilliant, and goofy. I'm the type of person who can read a comic book in the morning and an obscure book on deep metaphysics in the evening. I can hang out on a street corner one moment and with powerful movers and shakers the next. I can talk about the read option offense in pro football and the inner workings of the national economy the next. I can say without conceit that I could star in some "Most Interesting Man in the World" commercials. I'm formally educated with advanced degrees and yet my best education has come from simply living life. There are very few things I haven't either personally experienced or know someone who has experienced certain things. My life would make a very compelling movie.

      So who is Rom Wills? I'm a man who is on a mission to make a difference in the lives of the people I touch. Everything that I have experienced in life, good and bad, has been a life lesson. Through my writings, lectures, workshops, or talking trash in a barbershop I strive to share something that will positively impact the people around me.

Follow Rom on the World Wide Web:

www.romwills.com

Facebook.com/Willspublishing

Twitter: @RomWills1

www.ingramcontent.com/pod-product-compliance
Lightning Source LLC
LaVergne TN
LVHW051644080426
835511LV00016B/2475